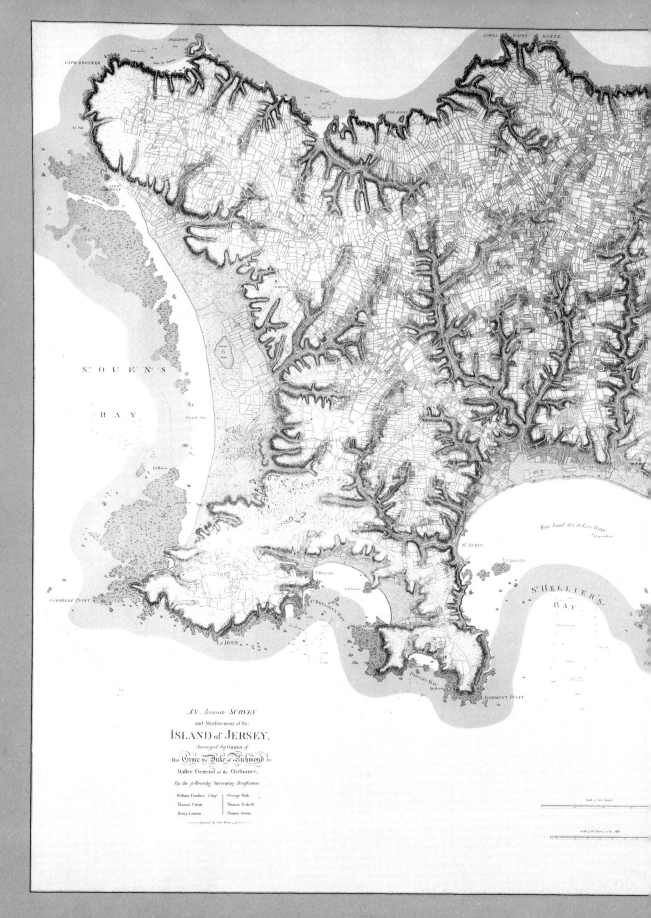

CAPE GROSNEZ

PLEMONT

SORRL POINT. RONEZ.

ILE AGOIS

St OUEN'S

BAY

Port de la Mare

La Rocco

La Corbiere

CORBIERE POINT

LA MOYE

St BRELADE'S BAY

St BOULSON

St AUBIN

St Johns Fort

Fine Sand dry at Low Water

St HELLIER'S

BAY

PORTLET BAY

NOIRMONT POINT

AN Accurate SURVEY
and Measurement of the
ISLAND of JERSEY,
Surveyed by ORDER of
His Grace the Duke of Richmond &c
Master General of the Ordnance,
By the following Surveying Draftsmen.

William Gardner Chief	George Pink
Thomas Cubitt	Thomas Yeakell
Henry Louran	Thomas Owens

Engraved by John Wear 1795.

Scale of 1000 Yards

Scale of 60 Chains or one Mile.

BERGERAC'S
Jersey

BERGERAC'S *Jersey*

JOHN NETTLES

Colour Photography by
KIM SAYER

Etchings by
MICHAEL RICHECOEUR

Published by BBC Books
a division of BBC Enterprises Ltd
Woodlands, 80 Wood Lane, London W12 0TT

First published in hardback 1988
First published in paperback 1991

ISBN 0 563 36178 6

Produced by Lennard Associates Ltd
Mackerye End, Harpenden
Herts AL5 5DR

Typesetting by Goodfellow & Egan
Design by Cooper·Wilson
Printed and Bound in Yugoslavia
by Mladinska Knjiga, Ljubljana

CONTENTS

FIRST IMPRESSIONS

When I arrived in Jersey in spring 1981, after years spent in the decent obscurity of the classical theatre, I must confess to being so absorbed in the hurly-burly of making the BBC's new series about a local detective called Bergerac that I took very little notice of the island itself.

Of the people I knew nothing: their speech was strange and their concerns were not mine, their way of life seemed alien. I lived in a hotel and spoke almost exclusively with the production crew and other actors. The work was arduous, fraught with the difficulties attendant upon a new venture, and I was plagued by doubts: would the series succeed or just disappear, like so many others? Was I the right actor for the job? Had I made the right choices in the characterisation? And so on and on.

I was not, therefore, in an ideal frame of mind to enjoy Jersey. I remember too that in those early days I was not actually over-impressed by the place. True, there was an abundance of pretty beaches, but then there was St Helier with its unprepossessing waterfront hiding, as I thought, a rather drab little town, notable for nothing so much as its labyrinthine and, to a visitor, impenetrable one-way system, its nondescript houses huddled together higgledy-piggledy, vulgar gift shops selling trash, and every night in high summer assorted drunks spilling from the loud and unlovely discotheques.

Once, long ago, some of the hotels had boasted a certain languid Edwardian charm, but they had been altered and 'developed' in the service of a crass commercialism which almost beggars belief but which was, and still is, an unnerving feature of island life. The whole town is crowned by Fort Regent. This had been an impressive military stronghold built between 1806 and 1814 during the Napoleonic struggles and named after the Prince of Wales who was also Prince Regent at the time. The fort was recently changed into a leisure complex, an extraordinary conversion that looks, particularly from the air, as if someone has pressed a huge ping-pong ball into the hilltop. It combines a marvellous ugliness with an embarrassing inability to please most of its patrons most of the time, as witness the endless correspondence in the excellent island newspaper, the *Jersey Evening Post*. It served us well, though, in the making of the series, providing us with a location for Diamanté Lil's nightclub and for many episodes which required large indoor spaces. But, the fact remains, it is not the most beautiful edifice on God's earth.

Then westward from St Helier to St Aubin and north towards Gorey, the broad bays were edged with scores of disparate Thirties houses and bungalows, many boasting 'improvements' in the shape of pseudo-Elizabethan fronts, pebbledash, stone cladding and, of course, green and purple roofs! Naturally, hotels and boarding houses figured prominently in this messy landscape and, since their main aim was to attract the custom of the passing tourist, their contribution to the quality of the environment was minimal. Everywhere, it seemed to me, from the holiday camp in St Ouen to the desalination plant in Corbière, the human architecture was at odds with the natural. I was definitely not enamoured of the island.

Now, seven years later, my view of Jersey is much altered. Filming here continuously since 1981, I have been able to discover, in my work and in my leisure, the hidden Jersey, off the beaten track and beyond the view of the casual tourist, an island of peculiar delight and infinite variety. The ugliness remains and, sad to say, has been added to in the intervening years but I have come to know those places in the island which still preserve what can only be thought of as the true and particular spirit of Jersey, epitomising that tradition of enlightened parochialism which is Jersey's own.

Still more important, I have found people, both indigenous and immigrant, who in their many different ways bring humour, love, light and enrichment to the life of this little island. It is to those people that this book is dedicated; I thank them for some of the happiest years of my life.

'What a pretty, rich country this is.' (*Queen Victoria, 1846*)

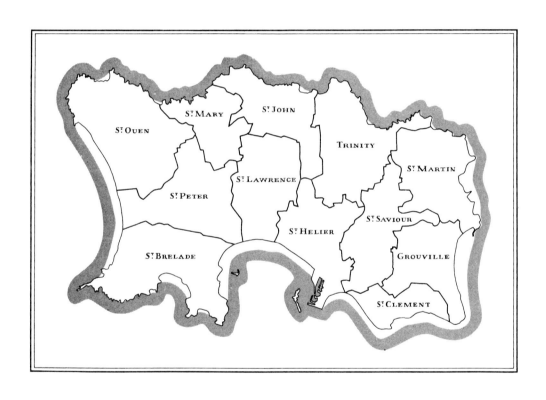

St Ouen   St Mary   St John   Trinity   St Martin   St Peter   St Lawrence   St Helier   St Saviour   St Brelade   Grouville   St Clement

A PECULIAR OF THE CROWN

The Bureau des Etrangers (department for non-residents) does not exist in Jersey; there is really no need for it to do so. It is nonetheless a delightful fiction and its so-called headquarters can be found at Haute de la Garenne, overlooking Grouville Bay.

The Bureau and indeed the character of Bergerac were conceived by Robert Banks-Stewart, a robustly extrovert Scot with an irreducible accent, known to his colleagues as 'The Laird'. He had been responsible for such series as the hugely popular *Shoestring*, with Trevor Eve. His unswerving instinct for commercial potential decided him to set his next series in Jersey, on the grounds that it was an extremely various island, exotic to a degree, apparently very rich with upwards of 80 millionaires amongst its 80,000 or so inhabitants, and that while it was in some ways exactly like mainland Britain in others it was entirely different. In short, he saw it as a potent mix of the familiar and the strange, where crimes of passion and crimes of greed might believably be committed.

Was it not likely that criminal elements might gravitate towards Jersey, attracted by its status as an off-shore tax haven? Might not drug barons from across the world launder their ill-gotten gains through the Jersey banks? Might not international arms-dealers ply their unseemly low-profile trade from somewhere relatively quiet like Jersey? Might it not be that all kinds of undesirables flourish and prosper in this beautiful isle?

The truth is that on the whole they do not, though there have been a few spectacular attempts to exploit Jersey's banking system in the last few years. I will return to this problem later in the chapter. By and large, it is fair to say that the facts – as usual – are at odds with the lurid imaginings of BBC scriptwriters. Even without a Bureau des Etrangers and a detective with a 99.9% clear-up rate, the States police manage to keep serious and petty crimes down to miniscule proportions.

The paid States police, a force begun in the 1850s, work side by side with the honorary, unpaid parish police who are known as centeniers. These officers have considerable powers, though it is true to say that with the increased sophistication of police methods that power has steadily diminished over the years, and the tendency now is to leave more serious and complicated police matters to the professionals. Nevertheless the centeniers embody the principles of voluntary, unpaid community service which characterise much of Jersey's public life and are enshrined in the practice of the Jersey Parliament, or the Jersey States as it is called.

None of the States representatives is paid, but the attendance record is exemplary and the quality of debate, mercifully free from party politics in the Westminster sense, is to my understanding very high indeed, always informed, sometimes passionate, often humorous and always caring. If you are in Jersey and would like to test the truth of that assertion, tune in to BBC Radio Jersey when they are broadcasting proceedings from the States. You will also hear the authentic Jersey accent which, somehow, you never hear on *Bergerac*!

Jersey has a special and time-honoured relationship with Great Britain. This was well summarised by the historian Philippe Falle who called the island 'a Peculiar of the Crown' but not a 'parcel of the Realm of England'. This is equally true of the other Channel Islands, although each manages its home affairs along individual lines.

ABOVE LEFT *Heart-throb Patrick Mower taking time off from stealing diamonds to seduce Cécile Paoli as Francine. Not only did he make Bergerac particularly jealous but this was also one of the few episodes in which the villain got away with the crime . . . but not the girl! Chris Fairbank (Moxey of* Auf Wiedersehen, Pet) *was not so fortunate (above) when he tried to hold Charlie Hungerford and the Bergerac family hostage. Happily this sort of thing is not a regular occurrence in Jersey.*

The islands are grouped in two Bailiwicks, those of Jersey and Guernsey, and the latter also includes Alderney and Sark. Each Bailiwick has a Lieutenant-Governor who is the Queen's representative. In Jersey the Lieutenant-Governor has a seat in the States assembly but may neither speak nor vote. The man who really runs the island is the Bailiff, and the current holder of that office is Sir Peter Crill, CBE.

As Bailiff, Sir Peter is at once Moderator, Speaker (as in the House of Commons), Chairman and paternal adviser. His power in the chamber is indirect rather than direct, displayed with discretion in a neutral, disinterested manner. As he once said, 'You do not express an opinion in the States, nor debate the workings of the States outside the chamber, but you can express a view on what is good government if there is a lack of cohesion and members need to be guided from time to time.' This is a characteristically modest appraisal of his role for he is in fact a very powerful figure in island affairs. I rather think that were he to come across Deputy Charlie Hungerford, Chairman of the Law and Order Committee, he would eat him for breakfast!

The Bailiff oversees a chamber composed of twelve senators. They are elected by the islanders for a period of six years. In addition there are twelve constables, or connetables, one from each of the twelve parishes, who are elected for three years, and twenty-nine deputies who are also elected for a three-year term (Charlie Hungerford is one of these). Because of the size of the island and the ratio of electors to elected, each member is well-known and must play a very open part in public life. Not only is the Jerseyman quite likely to know his States representative personally, if he meets him in the street or in a restaurant or pub he may well accost him on some issue of the day. It is this ease of access to the processes of government that is largely responsible for making Jersey such a pleasant place to live. Everyone can have a voice that can be heard, no-one need feel insignificant or dwarfed by the size of his environment. Jersey is built to a human scale, people can relate to the island and its institutions with ease without losing their own individuality. There are none of those violent destructive processes, generated by feelings of alienation, which are the curse of mainland inner-city life.

Not that the island is completely trouble-free, as we shall see. There are problems, and one of them, alcoholism, is very serious; the incidence of cirrhosis of the liver is four times greater than in England.

Other problems, of a criminal nature, are dealt with in one of two courts. Major offences are the responsibility of the Royal Court, and comparatively minor offences are dealt with by the Police Court. Sir Peter Crill, in his judicial capacity, administers the Royal Court assisted by twelve jurats (judges). It is in the Royal Court that, among other cases, charges of laundering money, handling drug profits and generally exploiting Jersey's special financial status within the United Kingdom are heard. These are very serious charges because they seem to call in to question the very integrity of the banking institutions which play a major part in Jersey's economy and, what is more, they threaten the constitutionally 'special' status which Jersey has enjoyed for so long with Great Britain.

Increasingly over the last five years, questions have been asked in both Houses of Parliament, allegations have appeared in the national press and highly critical programmes have been screened on television, all concerned with the possibility that millions of pounds of 'dirty money', particularly from drug-trafficking, is being laundered through Jersey. Senator Reg Jeune,who sits in the eye of this endless storm as President of the Finance and Economics Committee, vigorously defends the island's position. In 1988 he stated:

'The stature of the banks established in Jersey – nearly all of whom are banks in the world's top five hundred by size – together with the commitment of the authorities themselves, has ensured that Jersey has figured less prominently in the handling of the proceeds of drug trafficking, and certainly in the handling of cash, than other financial centres, including London . . .

'Whenever the laundering of the drug money through a Jersey bank is identified, every reasonable assistance is given to other enforcement agencies to bring those concerned to account. There are a number of ways in which this support is presently provided . . . The island's success in this endeavour is perhaps best summed up by quoting from a letter written recently to the Attorney-General by the Legal Attaché at the US Embassy in London: "You may rest assured that the FBI considers Jersey among our closest allies in combating illegal activities."'

BELOW LEFT *Alan MacNaughton and Susan Fleetwood (sister of Mick Fleetwood of Fleetwood Mac) in a splendid episode about an ex-Nazi hiding out in Jersey – two excellent performances. Perhaps more typical of Jersey crime was the story (below) involving Michael Gambon and Connie Booth in the laundering of money. This was the episode which I didn't finish because I broke my leg while filming – perhaps it was the competition from Gambon!*

The problem remains, however, and it will not easily go away. At the heart of Jersey's difficulties is this dilemma. How can the island's financial institutions allow investigative bodies access to their books without compromising that confidentiality which is an absolute condition of their continued, profitable existence?

I describe these matters at some length because at times, as I mentioned earlier, it does seem that the *Bergerac* series, for reasons of entertainment, presents the island in

*George Baker, as 'The Butcher',
in a controversial story,
powerfully written by John
Fletcher and set in London.
People complained about the lack
of Jersey content.*

a less than flattering light. That is almost bound to happen, however, given the underlying requirements of a police series set in a location as small as Jersey. At the same time, it is undeniable that in one or two areas of island life the fiction and the reality are not always so very far apart.

Jersey's essentially modern problems appear in strange contrast to the unchanging, old-fashioned character of the island's political and social institutions. Many of these date back with hardly a break to 1204 and are still going strong today. It is no accident that this book is built around the interlocking but very diverse stories of the twelve parishes. To a very great extent the parishes *are* Jersey, not just physically but in the way that everyday life revolves around them and their customs.

It is the parish authorities who still look after the island at local government level, and many signs remain of the old feudal style, symbolised by the seigneurial manor houses which dot the parishes, many of whose incumbents had extraordinary powers. Much of this power has become more centralised over the years: as we have seen, the honorary police have relinquished much to the paid States police force, and of course the old manorial courts – some of which had the right to hang convicted criminals – have yielded their role to the central courts in St Helier. Nevertheless the parish authorities, in the persons of the connetable (the parish police chief) the centeniers and the lesser vingteniers still exercise considerable power, as many an errant holiday-maker (or 'grockle', as they are called) has found to his cost. Moreover, as the local authority they are responsible for the maintenance of all the smaller roads or byroads within the parish, street lighting, a degree of policing, rubbish collection and the levying of rates. It is also noticeable to a newcomer that the general standard of service in all these is higher than in the UK, even if some of the officials work in eccentric ways.

Here is an example of how the law operates at parish level. If one is involved in a car accident of a non-serious nature, i.e. no-one is seriously injured, the law compels both drivers to present themselves to the local centenier at the parish hall so that he can assess culpability and damage. He has the power to decide if someone or no-one is to blame, whether there are mitigating circumstances and whether there should be a further inquiry, leading perhaps to a court appearance.

I was unfortunate enough, some years ago, to make such an appearance before the St Brelade centenier at the Salle Paroissiale at St Aubin. It happened like this. The track from my house came out on the main Corbière road at a point where the approach of traffic from the right was obscured by a sharp bend. Despite the aid of an old wardrobe mirror, held in place by chunks of stone and a quantity of string, getting onto the carriageway was always a hazardous affair.

One morning I was easing my newly acquired, second-hand, but to my mind beautiful Audi saloon onto the road when an ageing Ford Cortina hurtled round the bend. There was a noisy collision. I was not very pleased for two reasons. Firstly, my car was insured only for third-party, fire and theft and the damage amounted to £2,000; secondly (most unworthy reason!), the old Cortina, driven by someone I took to be a roughly dressed youthful hooligan, was completely unscathed.

By the time we appeared before the centenier the following Wednesday, the unkempt ruffian was transformed into a smartly dressed young man, clean-shaven and short-haired. He and the presiding centenier then conferred in polite Jersey tones about what had happened. I tossed in my version of events and awaited judgment. The old centenier in his tweed jacket, brown pullover and green tie, gazed mournfully with oyster eyes at an old-fashioned pack of Du Maurier and gave us reason to believe that he dated the decline of Jersey's culture, the decimation of the countryside and the increase in the incidence of lung cancer from the advent of the motor-car. We were plainly talking of things he hated. After some minutes in this vein of Spenglerian gloom he declared morosely that as far as he, and therefore the parish, was concerned, it had been an accident and consequently no-one was to blame.

The centenier's judgment was accepted by both parties. But, I said, could not something be done to minimise the risk of accidents on that bend. A sign saying, 'Slow. Concealed Entrance!' or perhaps a notice bearing the legend 'Special Care. Actor Crossing!' This last was an attempt to lighten the tone which I thought had become a little sombre. It was a mistake. The centenier sucked air harshly through his teeth, leant back in his leather chair, looked heavenward and delivered himself of the following piece of reasoning.

'John,' he said in a strangely forgiving tone, 'John, my boy, if I put up, or cause to have put up, a sign saying "Look out! There's a concealed entrance up ahead!" and you are driving home one day and you hit that sign, and that sign goes through your windscreen and hits you on the head and kills you, that sign could be considered a traffic hazard!'

Quite so. No sign was erected. Welcome to Jersey.

KEY DATES IN JERSEY HISTORY

BC
80000 — Cave people established in La Cotte, St Brelade.
AD
555 — Death of St Helier (Helibertus) who brought Christianity to Jersey.
931 — Jersey annexed to form part of Normandy.
1204 — King John loses Normandy; bailiwick system of self-government established in Channel Islands.
1461 — Jersey overrun by French; islanders endure seven years of tyranny.
1643 — Island under siege (until 1651) during English Civil War.
1771 — Code introduced defining Jersey's laws and roles of Court and States.
1779 — General Conway launches fortification programme for 30 coastal towers.
1781 — Battle of Jersey (see chapter 'St Helier').
1806 — Building of Fort Regent begun, completed 1814.
1846 — Queen Victoria visits Jersey; pays second visit in 1859.
1937 — Jersey airport opens; services transferred there from St Aubin's beach.
1940 — Jersey occupied by German forces, liberated on 9 May 1945.
1953 — Hague Court confirms Britain's ownership of the Minquiers and Ecrehous.
1981 — Sergeant Bergerac lands in Jersey.
1987 — October storms cause massive damage to trees and houses.

ST BRELADE

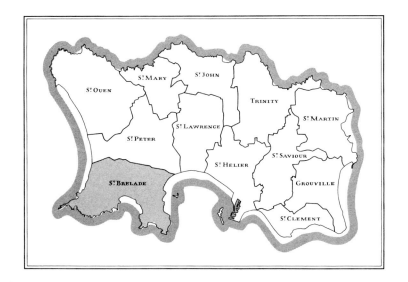

The parish of St Brelade is where I have lived since 1982 and it is the one I have come to know best. Were I not a rogue and vagabond actor, it's where a home would be ideal. However, as you can readily imagine, the pressure on housing in an island nine miles wide (east to west) and five miles long (north to south) is intense and the island fathers are at pains to enforce strict rules governing who can buy what and where.

A few extremely wealthy people, I mean multi-millionaires, are allowed in each year, simply on the basis of the proportion of their income which they make over to the coffers of the States of Jersey; for the common run of humanity, many years have to be spent in the island before permission to buy a house will be granted, and the whole process is hedged about with difficulties.

Being in what is termed 'J' category, which means I am 'essentially employed', I am allowed to rent or lease a house for the period of that essential employment, but no longer. It is a category sufficient to my needs, though, and when at the beginning of the second series of *Bergerac* I found 'Gorseland', it was all I wanted.

'Gorseland' is a sprawling bungalow standing in seventy acres of its own land on the headland that falls away to the much-photographed setting of the Corbière lighthouse. The desalination plant with its singularly unattractive chimney stack is also, alas, a near neighbour, but that's another story.

The bungalow is aptly named for it is surrounded by a great expanse of gorse alive with rabbits. At sun-up and sun-down they are to be seen, in large groups, standing still as stone, looking for all the world like a convocation of elders debating the more abstruse points of theology. A pair of hawks incessantly patrol the sky and during the long hot summers a pair of swallows nested in one of the adjoining garages which, for the length of their stay, we kept secure against unwanted predators.

Mela White, otherwise known as Diamanté Lil, in the bar of The Royal Barge. This was, in fact, a standing set in the old Forum cinema in St Helier.

When the summer birds go, they go suddenly and the year slips through the autumn to the winter months; truth to tell, this is when I find the island most appealing. The holidaymakers have disappeared and with them the all-pervasive smell of sweat and sun-tan oil; the endless queues of hire cars have gone too and the roads and lanes are relatively uncrowded; the beaches are empty and the wind whipping across the Channel and up over La Pulente burns your face with driven sand and assaults your nose with the pungent smell of vraic.

Vraic (pronounced *vrack*) is seaweed, and at one time it was vital to the island economy. Every six months, when it lay thick on the sands, it was hauled away to manure the fields. So important was it to the farmers, they would often turn St Ouen's (the biggest beach) into a battlefield as they fought over the rights to the precious stuff. It doesn't happen now, of course; riot and disorder are generally confined to St Helier a couple of times a year at closing time – or to certain more lurid episodes of *Bergerac*.

The parish of St Brelade has within its boundaries some of the most beautiful beaches in the Channel Islands, if not the whole of Western Europe. Alan Whicker, a somewhat travelled gentleman, once told me that he considered St Brelade's Bay, hammocked between Noirmont and Beau Port, one of the loveliest in the world. To see for yourself, stand to the Beau Port side of St Brelade's Church on a clear autumn day and simply observe the clean sweep of the sand, the translucent sea and the startlingly red granite cliffs out towards La Cotte. I would not dispute his judgment.

Directors of *Bergerac* have not been slow to exploit the visual attractions of the bay and its immediate surrounds. In one scene, I well remember speeding somewhat unsteadily on a jet-ski through crowds of swimmers at the water's edge, attempting vainly, yet again, to catch up with a diamond thief, prettily embodied by Liza Goddard, and being threatened with arrest by a real policeman as I fell to the sand.

'You,' he said. 'You have broken every damned rule in the book'.

He had the book there to prove it; and indeed I had, albeit unwittingly. There followed some hasty negotiations between the outraged official and the BBC location manager and, after the oil of diplomacy had been poured over the machinery of discontent, filming was allowed to continue. The result was some rather spectacular footage of Bergerac clinging desperately to the ski as he whizzed across an impossibly blue sea, disappearing in the blinding sun towards the high cliffs of La Cotte. Even if the stories in *Bergerac* are sometimes average, you can generally count on the scenery.

In real life things are slightly different, a little less ambitious. Nevertheless, if the weather is fine and the sea placid I enjoy getting out on the water. Being a little old for charging around in a speedboat and not having the skill to sail, I prefer to glide sedately about in a canoe, a therapeutic exercise if ever there was one and the best possible way to explore the prettiest stretch of coastline in St Brelade, if not the whole of Jersey. It runs from La Cotte south-eastward round Le Fret Point, past the beach in Portelet Bay, round Noirmont Point and then northward by Belcroute Bay to St Aubin's Harbour. There you can have a pint in the Old Court House, better known to television viewers as the Royal Barge, Diamanté Lil's old place (though you will not find parking there as easy as Bergerac seems to).

Portelet Bay has some fairly ugly developments on the cliffs above it, but is still rather beautiful and for all that boasts a very fine military tower on the Ile au

*Working boats, pleasure boats,
poorly boats and that could be me
in a favourite craft, small canoe
in the sunset at St Ouen's.*

End of the day boats and prettiest of all (right) sailing dinghies gliding home by Elizabeth Castle.

The exterior of The Royal Barge, more usually known as The Old Court House in St Aubin.

The Noirmont observation tower during the fight scene in which the stunt man was thrown onto the rocks. It may not look very steep from this angle but the ground does in fact fall away sharply. It was a particularly difficult stunt falling onto such rough terrain.

ABOVE RIGHT *Tony Pack, a real-life person, if not a Jersey native. He looks after the deckchairs on St Brelade's Beach and is known to take tea in his hut on the beach every afternoon – an unusual ritual these days.*

Guerdain, built in the middle of the bay in 1808, during the Napoleonic Wars. The Ile au Guerdain is sometimes called Janvrin's Tomb and the tower on it Janvrin's Tower, after a Captain Janvrin who in 1721 was buried there after dying of the plague aboard his ship. Janvrin's remains were later moved to St Brelade's Church.

The more vulnerable stretches of Jersey's coastline, essentially those without tall cliffs to act as a natural defence, are eloquent testimony to Jersey's troubled past. The idea of fortifying the island comprehensively by adding towers in strategic places was conceived by General Conway, Governor of Jersey in 1772–95; the work was begun in 1779.

The building of these towers (popularly known, though sometimes mistakenly, as Martello towers after the Italian Tower of Martella) continued well into the 19th century, long after the Napoleonic threat was over; Kempt and Lewis Towers in St Ouen were not completed until the late 1830s. Later, of course, the Germans in World War II did their best to turn Jersey into an impregnable fortress by means of extensive military installations. At Noirmont the two sets of defensive works, the Napoleonic and the German, can be seen almost on top of one another. From the earlier period, at the foot of the Noirmont headland, is the huge and impressive Tour de Vinde, erected around 1812. Nowadays it fulfils a more pacific role as a sea mark for shipping.

If you look up from the black and white painted tower the great German fortifications dominate the cliff, and for added realism guns have been dredged from the sea and mounted in the emplacements. There are no less than 18 German military installations on Noirmont Point including searchlight platforms, gunsites, personnel and flak emplacements. The conspicuous round tower which is the most southerly of the fortifications was a naval direction-finder post, and was the scene of a wonderfully choreographed fight sequence in one of the *Bergerac* films. At its climax the stuntman, Paul Weston, who now works on James Bond movies, was thrown from the top of the tower onto the rocks below – a very long drop indeed. I confess I could not watch!

Beyond the warlike Noirmont Point, towards St Aubin's Harbour, a more gentle and civilised seascape becomes apparent; here are delightful little coves with pleasant woodlands above them, and outcrops of rock just offshore crowded with seabirds. Altogether it engenders a marvellous sense of calm and peace, a peace which we managed to shatter one cold March day during the shooting of the very first episode of *Bergerac*.

Noirmont Manor, a beautiful house overlooking Belcroute Bay, used to be Charlie Hungerford's mansion and it was there that Bergerac went after his drying-out treatment in a London clinic to pick up his belongings and his beloved car. Charlie appeared wearing a yellow helmet and driving a massive earth-mover with which he was creating a new garden. The encounter between Hungerford and Bergerac was duly filmed and the earth-mover was parked some distance away from the house on a dirt road running round the edge of the wooded cliff.

Our famous digger that fell off the cliff onto the beach at Beau Port. The director said he was very sorry but when was the next one going to arrive. You can see what a terrible tragedy it would have been had there been people on the beach, as indeed there are during the summer months.

A teabreak was called and the entire unit; gathered round the tea and coffee urns in the courtyard of the manor – fortunately, as it turned out. Suddenly, from the direction of the dirt road came a terrible roaring sound. It was the earth-mover. Running to look, we arrived to see it hurtling down the cliff snapping off trees in its path like matchsticks. With a colossal bang the machine hit the retaining wall and fell, axles broken, crane arms twisted, and finished up spreadeagled on the beach below.

The first frightening thought was that Terence Alexander was in it, but he emerged quickly from the house to find out what was going on. Luckily no-one was anywhere near it at the time, and the reason for the accident remains a complete mystery. I was enormously glad that it happened on a cold miserable day in late winter, when the beach onto which this huge and lethal lump of metal had tumbled, was utterly deserted. On any fine summer morning it is always crowded, especially beneath the retaining wall.

Back in St Brelade's Bay, La Cotte is an archaeological site of great importance. It is, or rather was, a large cave where excavations earlier this century have discovered evidence of human habitation over a period of 80,000 years. It is believed that many thousands of years ago, during the great Ice Age when the woolly rhinoceros and the arctic mammoth walked the freezing land, and when Jersey was part of mainland France, man was already established in La Cotte.

From the excavations it appears that animals were driven over the clifftop to their death, and the carcasses then dragged into the cave and carved up for consumption – a highly efficient way of bringing meat to the family of primitive man. However, not everything in the cave was a model of neat household management. The inhabitants of La Cotte were forced to leave when the accumulated débris, bones, skulls and assorted bits and pieces filled up the cave to a level a few feet from the roof, making for a rather cramped lifestyle. There is a lot to be said for efficient waste disposal!

The clear and sandy beaches of St Brelade and Ouaisne (pronounced *Way-ney*) are hugely popular, and if it's solitude you're after, this is not the place to be, at least in high summer. I lived for some little while in a cottage near St Brelade's Bay Hotel, and the days were filled with the growls of over-large coaches disgorging the usual assortment of British holidaymakers onto the already crowded beaches, the smells of hundreds of meals being prepared in the many cafés and hotels, and the shrieks and howls of the myriad bathers splashing in the cool water – all, it seems, having a wonderful time.

I used to swim from St Brelade's in the early morning before the day's filming and I would marvel at how quickly the character of the place would change, with the arrival of the crowds, from a quiet backlit arena for a few joggers, the cleaners, four or five dog walkers and, glory of glories, a couple of horses being galloped through the surf, to a whirling kaleidoscope of running children, topless beauties, beefy torsoes and near-comatose elderly folk slumped in deck-chairs, tabloids protecting their frail heads from the sun. Out on the water were families in pedal boats, water-skiers, jet-skiers, surfers, wind-surfers, swimmers, paddlers and parascenders!

This is a scene from the very first episode with Cécile Paoli surrounded by extras, some of whom have become extremely well-known because they continue to reappear in the series. The lady to Cécile's left is remarkable in that she can cry on cue – something which even professional actors find difficult.

It can be all too much for the lover of quiet. Away, then, if you will, to the little Church of St Brelade which stands immediately on the side of the bay looking, it is hoped, benignly on all the summer mayhem.

I will always remember this church with particular affection for it was one of the first, and certainly one of the most photogenic, locations that we have ever used; also because, whenever I pass or visit it, I am reminded of Cécile Paoli who played Francine, Bergerac's first girlfriend whom, some say, he should never have lost. She was a lovely French girl, with long dark hair, brown eyes and a strong, very attractive accent. She would pronounce Jim as 'Jeem' and office as 'oafiss' (even if she could pronounce Bureau des Etrangers better than anyone in the cast), and she once reduced an entire crew to giggles when she imperiously ordered a 'prone cocktail' from the chuck waggon. Needless to say, her English was much better than our French and she bore our lumpen British humour with Gallic charm. She was a delightful companion and a memorable television presence, remembered with affection by many people. I shall always think of her as she was on that first cold March morning, nervous and beautiful, standing on the beach with the little church behind her, half hidden by the swirling spray and sand.

The Norman church at St Brelade dates from the 11th century, and because of its great age and because it is built of the local stone it seems to belong absolutely to the island; despite sometimes being overrun with tourists it retains, always, a tangible religious atmosphere. If you look at the sundial in the south transept you will find a salute to that old common arbitrator, Time, enough to lower the temperature on the hottest summer day. It is a quotation from Psalm 144, Verse 4: *L'homme est semblable à la vanité, ses jours sont comme une ombre qui passe.* (Man is like to vanity, his days are as a shadow that passeth away.)

Up until the Reformation every church in Jersey had a *perquage* or pathway to the sea along which felons who had invoked the *franchise de l'église* (the right to sanctuary in the church) might escape with impunity to the sea. Once a criminal had taken this route out of Jersey, he or she was never allowed to return to the island. The *perquage* for St Brelade's Church, one of the last two in existence (the other is at St Lawrence), can be found immediately outside the south door where a flight of stone steps leads down to the beach and so to the sea.

The production team from *Bergerac* have used the church and churchyard many times for scenes of burial and marriage. The church itself was broken into by a potential killer in an early episode, and more recently the parish hall, built of more sombre stone and standing immediately behind the church, served as the headquarters of a diabolical medium played by Barry Ingham in 'Fires in the Fall'.

In the everyday world the church generates a strong atmosphere of calm and security, and it was especially shocking to see its surroundings so utterly changed in the course of one night in October 1987 when the great storms crashed through the islands. Huge trees, seeming monuments to permanence, were flung headlong to the ground; everywhere around the church, and throughout the bay, was altered completely in that one night. If repeats of *Bergerac* do nothing more, they can at least remind us of the beauty that was and will not be restored in our lifetimes.

Barry Ingham, who gave us all great advice on how to succeed in Hollywood when he flew in specially to play a phoney medium.

Seaward from St Brelade's Church there is a path leading over the cliffs to the completely unspoiled beach of Beau Port (stouter hearts may attempt the way round the base of the cliffs at low water). It is the favourite beach for many a Jersey 'bean', as the locals are called. Favourite partly because of its seclusion, but mostly for its beauty and safe bathing. Charlie Hungerford once had the amazing and wonderfully vulgar notion of building a huge hotel complex on the valley leading to the beach and covering the whole bay with a retractable glass dome. This was to ensure that money was not lost because of adverse weather conditions! It was entrepreneurial thinking of a high order and, as he himself might have said, 'Not such a daft idea as all that, I mean look at the Americans and Disneyworld!' He dropped the idea because he lost his backers, but I think he also knew he would have difficulty getting permission for such a grandiose scheme from the Island Development Council which controls such matters.

Fortunately the terrain immediately surrounding Beau Port beach is fairly rugged and has been mercifully preserved from would-be developers; consequently, there is none of the clutter of cafés and shops you find in St Brelade's Bay. It is true that around the cliffs the authorities, in a concerted move to make the island look like an over-elaborate garden, have been 'prettifying' the place. The appearance of the car park has been improved by the erection of neat stone walls and there are cute little signposts telling you where you are going and, of course, lots of 'unsightly' undergrowth has been removed.

Performing this kind of cosmetic exercise is rather like an actor undergoing plastic surgery to achieve what he or she thinks is a more acceptable face, and thereby destroying that very individuality which is his chief asset. However, at the time of writing the reorganisation of Nature's handiwork is not that intrusive and most times in the middle months of the year, if you lug a hamper down the cliff, and bury your bottle of wine in the sand to keep it cool, you can have a wonderful day out on a completely unspoilt beach. Unless, that is, you are friendly with a certain actor, who shall be nameless, who took it into his head to buy a few bottles of champagne at Le Riches stores and bury them in the sand during the morning with a view to having a kind of 'bubbly hunt' in the afternoon. As it usually does, the tide came in and those bottles, for all I know, are still bobbing far out to sea or lie buried in unmarked graves, mourned and not forgotten.

Incidentally, a Jersey bean once told me that young men and boys used to leap, at full tide, from the top of the tall needle-rock standing to the right of the beach as you face the sea, as some sort of initiation test! The imagination boggles!

Beau Port, then, is an idyllic spot for a lazy day on the beach. If, though, during the nesting season, you swim out too far you may be mobbed by gulls protecting their offspring. On a few Sundays in high summer the bay is jammed with many little yachts and motor boats that have converged there from Guernsey, from mainland Britain, from St Helier just across St Aubin's Bay and from France. Sean Arnold, who plays the saturnine Chief Inspector Crozier and is possessed of an eagle eye for the main chance, has developed a way of wheedling liquid refreshment from the French yachting fraternity. His strategy is to swim alongside and call out in his best Franglais, 'Au secours, au secours! Je suis anglais mais je ne suis pas un football hooligan et j'ai

Sean Arnold looking secretive presumably as his alter ego, Barney Crozier.

ABOVE LEFT *Charlie Hungerford explains to a somewhat bemused Arab how he plans to put a glass dome over the whole of Beau Port Bay. Shortly after that scene someone tried to murder him. I am not surprised – it was probably the conservationists!*

besoin de quelquechose à boire!' Thus is begging made profitable and the *Entente Cordiale* secured.

If your taste inclines more to a quiet lunch and a gentle stroll afterwards, then may I suggest a visit to the Sea Crest Restaurant, just around the corner from the Corbière lighthouse at Petit Port. There you will be made royally welcome either by Victor, the owner, or by Sergio, the Maître d' who swears his surname is Parmesan! Whatever the truth of that, you may dine here excellently, as I do often, and then perhaps take a walk along the cliff path to La Pulente and St Ouen's beach.

The massive German bunker you will encounter, should you take this route, was opened up for our film crew to shoot a fight sequence between Bergerac and Warren Clark, who on this appearance in the series was a dastardly German film star. Curious though you may be about the interior of the bunker, which is privately owned and the entrance kept sealed, I can assure you it is a noisome, dark and depressing place. The most interesting thing we found was what looked like the remains of a party, *circa* 1965. Flowers had been painted on the wall together with a now barely decipherable litany of political slogans advocating a heady combination of free love, unilateral disarmament and folk singing as the panacea for the world's ills. Remember those naive days?

From that bunker between Petit Port and La Pulente, the whole sweep of Five Mile Beach becomes visible and a very impressive sight it is too, running south to north across the boundaries of three parishes, St Brelade, St Peter and St Ouen. Here you will find plenty of space to walk, talk, swim, surf or just lie down and sleep, but before you do any of these things look upwards from the beach at La Pulente and consider for a moment one of the most mysterious cases ever encountered by the Jersey police.

A film within a film. Bergerac watches as a visiting German film crew shoot a scene on the lawn of Charlie Hungerford's house. The film's director (played by Warren Clarke) was a German who had fathered a Jersey child during the occupation – a delicate subject for the island. It is greatly to the island's credit that such children were, in fact, accepted into the community very readily.

It concerns a couple living in a bungalow just beyond the hill that overlooks the beach. At the time of writing it has not been solved although the investigations at one time tied up sixty officers of the States force, involved the mainland police, the French police, a BBC *Crimewatch* programme, a helicopter, a Guernsey psychic and latterly the use of the most sophisticated radar equipment known to forensic science. Critics have said that the story-lines in *Bergerac* are sometimes far-fetched, but they do not begin to compare with this real-life drama.

The story begins in October 1987. At its centre are Nicholas Newall (aged 56) and his wife Elizabeth (48), who from all the accounts of those who knew them are, or were, a perfectly normal middle-aged couple, with no apparent personal problems; they have been variously described as a 'loving couple', as being 'well loved' and as a 'terribly happy pair, full of fun and life'.

Elizabeth Newall worked as a teacher, as Nicholas had done until a minor but recurring illness forced him to retire in 1983. They appear to have been very close, and enjoyed swimming, walking, and playing badminton and tennis together. They frequented the local restaurants at L'Horizon, the Sea Crest and the Lobster Pot, as do most middle-class Jersey folk. They were not especially wealthy but were comfortably off and spent several months of each year in Spain where they had a villa.

In 1987 they returned from that country towards the end of August and during the following month they made a number of trips out of the island, one to Sark, another to Portsmouth, one to London and one to Scotland. Each of these trips was undertaken so that they could visit members of their family. They returned to the island on 6 October and life seems to have proceeded quite normally: the usual shopping, and a visit to an optician – nothing to suggest that anything was out of the ordinary.

On Friday 9 October their two sons Mark and Roderick arrived in the island to visit their parents. On Saturday 10 October they lunched with their parents, then left in the early afternoon to return about 8 o'clock that evening for a family outing. Together, the Newall family drove the mile or so to the Sea Crest Restaurant, leaving about midnight for their home. After spending some two hours there the two sons left at about 2.30 am to spend the remainder of the night at Mark's property at Noirmont.

They returned at 8.30 am on the Sunday morning to their parents' home. At 9 o'clock a friend of the family called round, but as Nicholas and Elizabeth were still in bed she did not see or speak to them. Roderick and Mark wished their parents goodbye at 3 o'clock that afternoon and left, by air, for the mainland. That was the last time Nicholas and Elizabeth Newall were ever seen.

It was not until 17 October that the alarm was raised when a friend of the family, worried by her lack of success in getting in touch with the Newalls, telephoned the next-door neighbour, Mr Michael Shearer. He entered the Newalls' house and found no-one. Roderick and Mark returned immediately to the island, understandably concerned for the welfare of their parents, and that afternoon reported to the police that Nicholas and Elizabeth were missing.

According to police reports the bungalow showed no indication that anything untoward had happened. There was food on the table and some newspapers lying about, though none dated after 10 October; there were some packing cases in the back which included various items the Newalls would need when they next travelled to Spain. They had planned to depart on 20 October, and a passage was booked for that date on the ferry to St Malo, from where they would drive into Spain. Their passports were found in the house, however, and it was later established that the couple had certainly not been on the ferry when she sailed on 20 October.

There are other, more mystifying features to the case. Apparently, the timing-clock on the central heating had been bypassed, which meant that the heating was running continuously for twenty-four hours a day. Added to that, the thermostat was on maximum heat – unusual for a mild autumn. As far as could be ascertained from a search of their wardrobes, the only clothes missing were those which the couple wore on their visit to the Sea Crest on 10 October. The inference was, therefore, that they were wearing those same clothes when they disappeared. As detectives pointed out, if the couple had simply gone out for a walk they would certainly not have worn such formal clothes.

What has happened to them? Is it possible, on the small island of Jersey, for two people to disappear so utterly and completely? Apparently, and sadly, the answer is yes. On 28 October, the head of Jersey CID, Detective Chief Inspector Martyn le Brocq made the following statement: 'This continued disappearance is as baffling for us as it is distressing for the family.' Despite the fact that a subsequent statement suggested that the case was nearing a satisfactory conclusion, nobody was arrested and the Newalls remained missing.

Six months later, the mystery was no nearer solution although a number of clues uncovered in the meantime appeared to suggest that this was no voluntary disappearance. Police tracker dogs found certain personal items on an unnamed site on the north coast.

Further scrutiny of the bungalow revealed two spots of blood and evidence that someone had made a 'determined attempt' to clean the place up; this was probably why the heating had been running at full blast – to dry up the water used. These and other pointers have in themselves proved nothing, but each one increases the conviction in the mind of every islander that: 'It must be murder.'

ST PETER

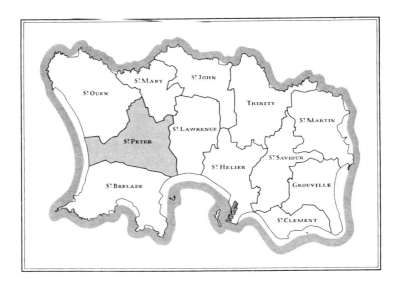

For thousands of visitors the first sight of the island is from the air as they fly in, either from the west over the Channel between Guernsey and Jersey or from the east from the coast of France. In the very first episode of our series it was via Jersey Airport that James Bergerac arrived back to an uncertain future after an accident to his leg.

In the opening flying sequence there was a massive mistake in continuity. The plane that took off was not the same plane that landed, so Bergerac achieved in the first five

minutes of the series the remarkable feat of changing planes in mid-air. If his ability as a detective could equal his gift for sleight of hand, the man clearly had nothing to worry about.

Before the airport was built in St Peter's, air services to the Channel Islands and to London were run from St Aubin's beach, the aircraft paying habour dues which seems peculiarly logical. Of course, the beach is tidal and this meant that aircraft could only land and take off at certain times which varied from day to day depending on the state of the tide. As Alistair Layzell records in his excellent book *Announcing the Arrival*, the pilots, to save precious time, very often did not leave the cockpit while the aircraft were first unloaded, then fuelled and reloaded.

As a travel courier Francine's work often took her to the airport and we shot many scenes there. As you can see from the rag-bag with the string tie, at this particular point in time neither I myself, nor the wardrobe department had worked out a dress-style for Bergerac.

In 1932 the States opted for the present site of the airport. There was the usual problem of persuading the incumbent farmers to part with their precious vergees of land, which became even more precious when it was learned that the States wanted them; but eventually the necessary land was purchased and work commenced. On 10 March 1937 Jersey Airport was opened by Mrs Babs Coutanche, wife of Bailiff Alexander Coutanche. It has since become one of the busiest airports in the United Kingdom.

During the war, it was used by the Germans and there is a lovely story of how Charles Roche, an Englishman who remained in the island to run the airport at the beginning of the war, managed to have the grass runways cut to below their proper height. This had the effect of preventing the wheels of incoming aircraft from gaining a hold on the ground, and so they would slide about and even crash. Unfortunately for Mr Roche, and for the Allies, this excellent administrator was sent to an internment camp in 1942.

Since the war the airport has been expanded to cope with the ever-increasing influx of tourists and freight from all parts of the UK and Europe. It still has, of necessity, a relatively short runway and the larger jets on regular UK routes often have to use reverse thrust on landing. If the traveller is not forewarned of this procedure, as he sometimes is not, arriving in the land of sunshine and early potatoes for the first time can be a hair-raising experience. On one type of aircraft the rear cowling on the wing-mounted jet engines is lowered on landing to act as a brake. I did not know this fact in the early days, and when I first saw it I thought the engine was falling off and prayed hurriedly that my burgeoning career would not be cut off in its prime.

There was, and is, no cause for alarm about this odd procedure. Of late there has not been an accident worth the name at the airport. There have been, however, delays caused by the fog, and in 1987 there was a terrible jam of people waiting for planes that could not operate because of an extended period of minimal visibility. Literally thousands of people were left hanging about the place until the weather improved, which thankfully it soon did. Questions were asked in the States as to what could be done to alleviate the distress of travellers so stranded, but the plain truth is that mist and fog are endemic to island life, and beyond making certain that adequate facilities for sleeping are available, there is precious little that the authorities can do to improve things.

The airport, by virtue of its size, is the dominant feature of the parish of St Peter, and for that reason it is by far the noisiest parish. I cycle past it regularly to get down the narrow lanes to St Ouen's Bay, and the pungent smell of raw aerofuel in the air is reminiscent of the freeways to and from Los Angeles Airport. Having never lost a somewhat childish delight in watching heavier-than-air machines take off, I often stop with many other like-minded people to watch from very close quarters as the UK-bound jets shoot into the sky. I then return to my travels on a more humble mode of transport.

Being interviewed on location for the BBC magazine programme Look Now. *The setting is St George's House, frequently used in the series.*

To the north of the airport is the Val de la Mare Reservoir. The walk along its southern edge is very pleasant indeed and, when the airport is not too busy, beautifully quiet. If, from the village of St Peter, you go north along the Grand Route de St Pierre, a car park can be found at the head of the flooded valley; from here the path leads all the way down to the the great dam facing out towards St Ouen's Bay. The views are spectacular.

From the dam itself you can look out across the Sunset Nurseries in the deep valley below to La Rocco Tower which stands on a rock offshore and is the dominant feature

One of the large houses above St Peter's Valley. Jack Higgins, the novelist, has a house nearby.

of St Ouen's Bay. During the last war it was used by the Germans for target practice. A local Jerseyman who had lived through that time told me that they must have been lousy shots for the tower, as it was in the Fifties, owed its ruined state much more to the depredations of time and the sea than to exploding shells. The tower was restored in 1969, a belated beneficiary of the growing awareness that the island's heritage was important and must be cared for.

St Peter's is an unassuming little parish but it contains several delightful spots, the most beautiful being St Peter's Valley. It was through this valley that Sir John Le Couteur took Queen Victoria when she paid a second visit to Jersey in 1859. The Queen, on impulse, had decided to return briefly to the island that had so royally received her some 13 years previously. She went to see Victoria College, named after her and still a famous seat of learning in the island. She sailed by yacht to St Aubin and from there Sir John, her ADC and a most accomplished Jerseyman, drove her in a carriage through what he believed was one of the most beautiful valleys in the island.

Apart from its quietly impressive natural beauty, the Valley boasts a lovingly restored 600-year-old watermill, Le Moulin de Quétivel, which was brought back into

One of the ubiquitous Jersey arches. This is a relatively plain example. For more ornate versions see those at Mont Orgueil and Elizabeth Castles and best of all the arch at Longueville Manor.

A more modern and pretentious gateway. Charlie Hungerford would covet this.

FACING PAGE *Old farm building built of the beautiful pink Jersey granite which is now highly expensive.*
LEFT *The hall of St Ouen's Manor, in the centre a portrait of Charles II.*
BELOW *A rather impressive farmhouse.*

LEFT *Some of the more pleasant houses in St Helier.*
ABOVE *The pub-cum-club on the 'Minkies' where many a noggin's been drunk.*

Riding out along the Jersey lanes.

service during the grim Occupation years. It is now the property of the National Trust for Jersey and is as wonderful an evocation of the island's past as you will find anywhere.

There is, too, the Strawberry Farm, which though it could never be said to be attractive is nevertheless of great historical interest. It was the site of the German Command Headquarters. Aerial photographs exist which show how the military installations were painted and disguised to look like innocuous farm buildings. One of the bunkers, similar to that on the Hougue Bie site, is open to the public. The Strawberry Farm is a tourist delight, combining as it does a warlike past with a more peaceful present in the shape of a local craft centre and a model village.

The *Bergerac* unit has filmed in and around several houses in this secluded valley and, to my mind, they are among the most beautiful in the island. One house I remember particularly well. When we arrived to film, the owner, a frail elderly lady, had been taken away to spend the remainder of her days in hospital. Her house was packed with unfashionable, impressive Edwardian furniture, and there were the sad remains of what had clearly been a wonderful conservatory off the dining-room; everywhere there were photographs, pictures, prints and small statues, extraordinary if not for their quality then for their profusion. It was a very 'lived-in' house, and we worked there for two days. Our designer, then as now, Phil Roberson, one of the best kind of BBC personnel, talented and unobtrusive, pointed out a strange fact about this wonderfully ornate residence. Nowhere in the twelve or so rooms is there a single picture, photograph, print or statue of any male figure. The lady, we assumed, was a feminist.

The Cowman

ST OUEN

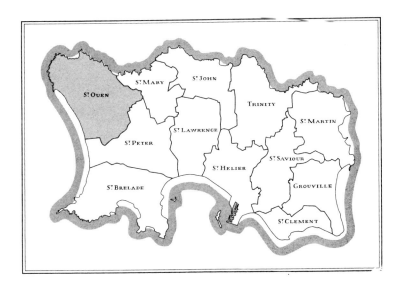

Bounded to the west by part of Five Mile Beach and to the north by the tall forbidding cliffs of Les Landes, St Ouen is the most individual of all the parishes. It is the home of the de Carteret family and retains a strange, brooding melancholic air as if suffering from the weight of its often hard and turbulent past. The countryside is bleak, the coastline harsh and threatening. The houses, particularly those in the north, are functional rather than grand, and seem to crouch to avoid the fierce winds that rush across the broad treeless land between Grosnez and L'Etacq.

On that bare headland you will find memorials to the German Occupation littering the cliff-tops: great gun-towers and emplacements, bunkers and stores, many defaced with political and sexual obscenities courtesy of the spray can and youthful ignorance. It is amazing that these wartime hulks, monuments to man's inhumanity to man, should have been left to assault the spirit and ruin the countryside, but there they have remained for more than forty years.

A more aesthetically pleasing military structure lies at the north-west tip of the island: Grosnez Castle. Not much of it remains, merely the ruined gatehouse and the defensive ditch to its front and the foundations of a few small buildings inside the perimeter. The castle was built in the 14th century to provide a stronghold against the persistent and lethal raiders from France. It did not survive long, very likely because it was too small and inadequately fortified.

It does, however, look very impressive on film, which is why in one of our episodes Bergerac was seen pursuing a terrorist and would-be assassin through the ditch on the landward side of the wall and out towards the cliffs near the German observation tower; here the terrorist met his end. Not, however, before he had described Jersey as a

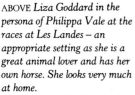

ABOVE *Liza Goddard in the persona of Philippa Vale at the races at Les Landes – an appropriate setting as she is a great animal lover and has her own horse. She looks very much at home.*

ABOVE RIGHT *In this episode two young surfers are just about to discover the body of a skin-diver on the beach at St Ouen's – not a frequent occurrence. You can get into trouble with the current but you don't usually drown. There were, as you might expect, strange circumstances surrounding this particular accident.*

'dump' and a haven for ne'erdo-wells and tax-dodgers, a description which aroused a good deal of anger in at least one person's breast. The offended party fired off a letter to the *Jersey Evening Post* questioning the value of continuing a programme which gave such bad publicity to the island.

Less murderous was the story involving the Ice Maiden (Liza Goddard), the impudent, clever, not to say lovely diamond thief, who forever makes Bergerac look two bricks short of a load, which we filmed largely at Les Landes racecourse close to Grosnez Castle. There are many meetings here during the year, both flat and steeplechase, and when the weather is fine there's no finer day out than Jersey races. I say when the weather is fine for there are times when the mist sits so tightly to the ground you would not know which horse was leading until it emerged from the vapoury gloom a few strides from home. It affected our filming, too; one day the cameraman had to give up because he could not see what he was supposed to shoot!

A local horse, Mr Chas, was the star of our show, entitled 'A Horse of a Different Colour'. Despite having to play a gay racehorse, Mr Chas acted to perfection and looked magnificent. The BBC crew became extremely fond of him, and when he ran at the next Bank Holiday meeting we collectively had £400 on him. Knowing that he had won every race he had entered, we crowded to the rails to cheer home our winner. He came last, and his owner disarmingly said (for it is a terrible thing to part a BBC person from his money) that this less than excellent performance was probably caused by our filming, which had interrupted his training schedule.

Another horse figures dramatically in one of the most famous tales of the parish. Some time between 1460 and 1470 when the French occupied most of the island, Philippe de Carteret, Lord of St Ouen, was out fishing in a lake near the beach when suddenly he saw a group of Frenchmen creeping up on him. He hurled himself onto his horse and fled for his life. Later, an appropriately anonymous rhymer described it thus:

DE CARTERET'S LEAP

The Lord of St Ouen was down by the lake,
When the sun through the mists was beginning to break.
By its margin he sought the bright finny race
To ensnare the bold pike or the silvery dace,
From the depths of its waters, so calm that the air
Scarcely rippled the surface, a mirror so fair.
The day is too chill, mists are floating so high,
Drawn from out the dark earth, to obscure the bright sky
Ah! Who are those creeping beneath that high mound
Of glittering sand, with a silence profound?
Oh, Lord of St Ouen's, I bid thee beware,
And fly from a deep and treacherous snare;
The foe will surround thee, thy blood on their steel
Will bedew the cold ground. Is there nought to reveal
The danger that threatens? His steed loudly neighs,
As corselet and falchion gleam bright in the rays
Of the sun, which now breaks thro' the mist and the gloom,
That may light with its beam on De Carteret's tomb.
Mount thy steed and away! Now he's off with a bound
From the foes who had sought Ouen's Lord to surround.
There's a race for a death, there's a race for a life.

Will the steed drink his breath in the mad'ning strife?
He's away to the hills – they are closely behind;
He ascends the steep bank, but new dangers to find.
On its brow there are foes, to cut off his retreat;
He bears himself bravely, his steed's strong and fleet,
To the vale of the Charrière he turns him aside, –
On! On! the foes follow, their steeds deeply dyed
With blood on their flanks, as they're goaded along,
He'll be slain, though his horse is so fleet and so strong
Too closely they follow – he'll ne'er reach the vale!
Of his death to his friends who will bear the sad tale?
Deep barks line the road, two and twenty feet wide –
He is lost, or across the deep chasm must ride.
Now aid him, brave steed, though thy heart may be broke,
Save thy Lord in his need from the falchion's stroke.
One spring! He bounds over! Alas, he is lost!
No! His steed gains his footing – in safety he's crossed.
Now hie thee, brave horse, o'er the long sandy plain;
On his castle de Carteret looks once again,
Ere he reaches its portal the gallant steed falls,
Yields his breath for his lord, who is safe by his walls.

Grosnez Point or 'big nose' seems an appropriate name for this promontory. You can see how inaccessible the coast is with its formidable natural defences.

There is an interesting epilogue to this story. In the first decade of this century, while improvements were being made to the garden around the manor house, some bones were discovered in the spot where it was thought that Philippe's trusty horse was buried. One of the bones was sent to the British Museum for analysis. The museum's investigation showed that it was a bone from a horse dating back more than four hundred years. Was this the de Carteret wonder horse? I like to believe that it was. The relic now lies in state in the main hall of the family manor.

Over the years the BBC, thanks to the kindness of the present Seigneur of St Ouen, has used the manor house and its grounds many times. It is one of the most impressive buildings in the whole of the Channel Islands, and for our purposes has

A rare trip to Alderney which is standing in for Chaussey in the SPARTA episode. Judy Buxton is the lovely actress doing the painting.

served as the residence of the eccentric millionaire, Sir Maxwell Flagg, whose misfortune it was to be robbed by the Ice Maiden; as an art gallery and museum in a very early episode with Warren Clarke and Linda Marshall (now more famous as the writer Linda la Plante); as a French château, in a somewhat far-fetched episode of the 1987 series concerning some rather hot-blooded French swordsmen, and as the headquarters of a ruthless neo-fascist, Sir Phillip Hanmer. In that episode, called 'S.P.A.R.T.A.', one of the spacious chambers in the manor was supposed to be a room in Fort Clonque in Alderney which in turn was supposed to be on Chaussey, a vertiginious juxtaposition of reality and illusion which confused me a lot, and I am in it!

However fanciful the stories our scriptwriters have dreamt up, nothing quite compares in variety, wonder and eccentricity to the real events which make up the history of the de Carteret family. At least as old as the Norman Conquest, the family became prominent in Jersey affairs in 1204 when the then Seigneur of St Ouen decided to throw in his lot with the English King John, even though this meant losing

FAR LEFT *Philip de Carteret and his wife at home, but in an unusually formal pose for a friendly and hospitable couple who are never known to stand on ceremony.*

LEFT *Sir George de Carteret, a great supporter of the Royalist cause.*

FAR LEFT *St Ouen's Manor is used as a setting for another Bergerac story. This picture shows the many architectural styles that make up the manor, parts of which date back before the 13th century. The chapel (left) is, on the other hand, a delightfully simple and private family chapel.*

ABOVE *The gatehouse at St Ouen's Manor, the first view that most visitors see as they arrive.*

I often cycle up to L'Etacq for this marvellous view of St Ouen's Bay. There are usually hundreds of swimmers and surfers on the beach looking, from this distance, like so many seals bobbing around in the foam.

all his lands in France because that hapless monarch had contrived to lose Normandy. From that time the de Carteret name appears on almost every page of the island's history, and in one remarkable instance during the 17th century it echoed far beyond Jersey and all around the western world.

George de Carteret (1608–80) was an extraordinary man. At various times in his life he became Bailiff of Jersey, Lieutenant Governor of Jersey, a high-ranking and famous officer in the Royal Navy, commander of one of the last outposts of Royalist resistance, Elizabeth Castle, a pirate, preying on Channel shipping, a ship designer of note, Treasurer of the Royal Navy (Samuel Pepys was his secretary), a privy councillor and a prime mover (though not entirely for philanthropic reasons) in the founding of the New World colonies of Carolina and New Jersey.

He was a firm supporter of the Royalist cause and Charles II repaid his loyalty during the years of exile with high office after the Restoration. The King also saved him from almost certain impeachment when de Carteret was mistakenly accused of mismanaging naval funds during his term of office as Treasurer of the Navy. In this he was fulfilling a promise made to de Carteret in 1649. It appears in the form of a postscript to a formal letter concerning the exchange of hostages with the Parliamentary forces. The letter and postscript are miraculously extant and can be seen at the manor. The postscript reads: 'Carteret, I will add this to you under my own hand, that I can never forget the good services you have done to my father and to me, and if God bless me you shall find I do remember them to the advantage of you and yours: and for this you have the word of your ever-loving friend, Charles R.'

Sir George de Carteret's later years may have been troublesome but this was the man who, in earlier days, might have altered the entire course of British history. In 1641, when the whole of Britain was on fire over the enmity between King and Parliament, Captain de Carteret was offered the position of Vice-Admiral of the Fleet, to serve under Admiral Warwick, a known Parliamentary sympathiser. At the behest of Charles I, de Carteret turned down what in other circumstances would have been a glorious advancement. His reason is not far to seek – he was a Royalist and he obeyed his King, it was as simple and straightforward as that. If, however, he had taken up the appointment, it is possible, or so the historian Clarendon believed, that with his charismatic reputation and enormous ability de Carteret might have mobilised the fleet on the King's side during the war to come. History is, of course, full of endlessly fascinating 'ifs' and perhaps to pursue them is a fruitless exercise; nevertheless one cannot help wondering what might have happened if Charles had had at his disposal the great weapon of the Royal Navy. At least in the early days of the war, might it not have swung the balance decisively in favour of the Crown?

The present 'Lord' of St Ouen is a splendidly down-to-earth man, Philip Malet de Carteret. Ten years ago he just managed to gather together sufficient money to purchase the manor house from his brother Rex, who was on the point of selling it to resolve his own financial problems. Since then Philip has battled to maintain the house and its extensive and beautiful gardens with a staff of two and no aid from the States. It has not been, he admits, at all easy.

By profession a stockbroker he has used, and still uses, his income from that source to keep up the expensive estate. Almost every week of the year he has to make painful decisions over whether, for example, it is better to have a painting cleaned or the roof repaired, there not being enough money to do both at the same time. He recalls how in the early years, with no adequate heating in many parts of the rambling house, he and his wife replied to a mail-order advertisement in a newspaper and invested in quantities of thermal underwear to keep themselves warm and the fuel bills down. He had a wood burner installed in the main hall and appointed himself to chop up the wood needed to fuel it. Having the use of only one eye, he found it difficult to hit the iron wedges used to split the logs; he returned to the advertisement columns of the newspaper, bought a chain saw and solved his logging problems.

Philip de Carteret has devoted his life and fortune to St Ouen's Manor and the people of Jersey have just cause to be deeply grateful to him. It is all too easy to envisage what might have become of the old place had it fallen into the hands of, say, a gang of hoteliers or developers.

JERSEY LA NUIT

If this bleak and wind-battered parish seems an odd place in our narrative to introduce the heady joys of Jersey night-life, do not be put out. This island is crammed with incongruities, which may be why St Ouen contains among its delights the Pontins Holiday Village and a couple of those painted dugouts, desolate by day, neon-lit by night, which wink at evening drivers on the Five Mile Road. To the north, meanwhile, in the otherwise tranquil seaside village of Grève de Lecq, stands the emperor of them all – Caesar's Palace.

I should first explain that one of the delights of my off-duty life is going out to see the current entertainment in the clubs and nightspots of the island, though sadly they are now much fewer than they used to be. I love and admire the talent and courage of comics, singers and dancers who often in badly designed venues and sometimes with inferior material battle on night after night to win over an audience, and never give up even when the odds are stacked against them. I recall the brave Scot, dressed in leather shorts and accompanying himself on a piano accordion, who performed an unlikely programme of Tyrolean music to an uncomprehending audience in one of the louder pubs. I remember too a club where a dancer did a high leap, for which the stage was manifestly unsuited, and knocked himself unconscious against the ceiling.

Two ladies take an evening stroll beside St Ouen's Bay – might they be on the way to the Château de Plaisir or some other neon-lit attraction on the Five Mile Road?

In that particular club there was little if anything to praise about the cabaret. When you walked through the door the sweet smell of mediocrity hit you like a freight train, a combination of sweat, cigarette smoke, beer and very strong disinfectant. The place has now closed down and I shall miss it. I remember, too, the stage catching alight in the middle of Stan Boardman's act at the Inn on the Park. Most of all, I remember a great comic playing one of his last weeks at Swansons, the music hall in St Helier.

It happened when we were making the first series of *Bergerac* and I could walk the streets of the town without being recognised. In search of a drink, a sit-down and a spot of entertainment I dropped into the upstairs bar of Swansons, overlooking the stage. It was a smashing show, I fell in love immediately with one of the dancers, admired the singing of Ruby Murray and I was enthralled by the comic. His material was completely original and his timing exquisite; he was unmistakably one of those great comedians possessed, like Les Dawson or Tony Hancock, of a comic persona which made the simplest observation, the smallest flick of the eye, hysterically funny. It was not simply an act, it was a celebration. I soon discovered that it was no less a person than Sandy Powell standing there on that diminutive stage, rocking them in the aisles. Time and again I returned to that show with actor friends to learn what we could of the great man's technique and to revel in his performance. It was a privilege I shall not forget. Swansons, by the way, is still open for live entertainment during the summer season.

At Grève de Lecq the parishes of St Ouen and St Mary meet, and there you will find a cultural clash of the centuries to relish: no less a spectacle than Napoleon Bonaparte versus the Last Nights of the Roman Empire. Above the beach, on the eastern or St Mary's side, stands a low, austere line of barracks, built in Napoleonic times to accommodate 150 men when the fear of a French invasion was paramount in Jerseymen's minds. In 1972 the National Trust for Jersey restored the barracks and in one room visitors can see how the soldiers lived and slept. Uniforms hang against the walls, the bed frames are bare iron, the bases an uninviting mesh of army string, the ablution blocks at the back of the building a monument to cold-water hygiene.

Should the chilly atmosphere of pre-Victorian plumbing give you goosepimples, banish further thoughts of discomfort by stepping immediately across the road into a steamier, flabbier world. Wallet at the ready, saunter past mute lions and a moody plaster Venus into the foyer of Caesar's Palace, 'Jersey's Most Lavish Nightspot'. This is the heart of the Dick Ray empire, complete with imitation Greco-Roman statues and busts, screwed-down tables and chairs and a commodious bar area with a fountain. The whole extravagant ambience could best be described as Byzantine-Ersatz or perhaps Jersey Baroque. One thing for certain, it's a great night out if you like that kind of thing. Since, for various reasons, I do, and so do many of my actor-colleagues and friends, I have spent many a happy night there hooting the comics, ogling the dancers, who are extremely pretty, and enjoying the lager and that cuisine-in-a-basket which they do so well at Caesar's Palace.

My favourite performers are the singers Stuart Gillies and Di Cousins. She is a very good, very Welsh middle-of-the-road singer who has become a regular at Caesar's. She is one of those entertainers I mentioned earlier who, no matter what the audience, will work on them until they are on her side and enjoying themselves hugely. I have never seen her fail in this and I have witnessed her performing in some of the 'hardest' places in Britain, such as Salford and Glasgow. So, if you too like down-to-earth, straightforward entertainment, take a night out at Grève de Lecq – and a taxi home.

L'Etacq

ST MARY

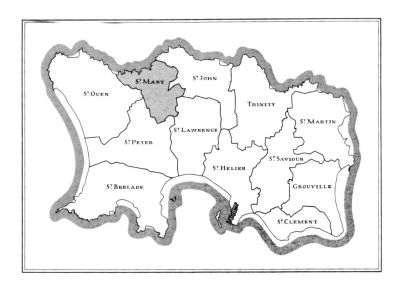

W alk the coastal cliffpath of this northern parish on a windy day and you soon grasp the rude aptness of the names applied to the local landmarks, especially the coastal protuberances and inlets: Red Nose (*Rouge Nez*), The Donkey (*L'Ane*) and Devil's Hole, for which a number of ingenious French origins have been suggested.

This is cave country, where for thousands of years the tides have burrowed into the cliff faces and created many of Jersey's three hundred caves. Devil's Hole is undoubtedly one of the most spectacular, though a little disappointing for the visitor who is no longer encouraged to climb down into it.

The hole appeared when the sea found its way into the back of an existing cave by another route, carving a jagged tunnel which early attracted the name *Creux de Vis*, or Screw Hole. While the centuries passed, and the sea noisily lapped and sucked its way through the cave, and at high tide shot clouds of spume and spray out through the rear entrance, fertile Jersey minds sought even more vivid names for it. The Rev. G. R. Balleine, the island's most prolific

historian, attributes the name Devil's Hole to an unknown charabanc driver, more literate than some, who connected an old Jersey nickname for the Devil – 'Le Vier Vi' – with the 'screw hole' in the cliff, and thereby, it is charitable to hope, greatly increased the number of tourists he could lure there for an afternoon's enchantment.

A rival theory has it that the original Devil was the figurehead from a wrecked Viking ship which was washed ashore near the cave, and refused to go away until it had frightened the natives into naming the place after it. A more recent figurehead story claims that in 1851 the effigy came ashore after a French ship was wrecked nearby, and somehow become lodged in the cave. A local sculptor was called in, and he restored the torso and added Satanic limbs to complete the legend.

Today, when you visit Devil's Hole, you go down a steep path from the Priory Inn, and there on the right, rearing from a slimy pond, is a statue of the Devil. Well, statue is perhaps overdoing it: this leering figure reminds me more of a pantomime villain, black and 'orrible with horns and a trident, leaning faintly backwards on his stand in the pond as though recoiling in horror from shouts of 'Oh, yes you did!' from an invisible child audience.

Such is Jersey nowadays, you may think I am saying. Lots of bad taste and too many tourists. At Devil's Hole, it has to be said, popularity has spoiled the place. Now you must view the hole from a gallery some way up the cliff; a few years ago, steps led all the way down to the entrance and you could walk into the cave, but the steps crumbled and became dangerous. At least, though, you are spared the spectacle of a second Devil, a brother of the one in the pond, which used to lurk down in the hole. After the owners had lost a couple of Devils washed out to sea, they gave up the idea; it must count as an improvement.

The Priory Inn is also a good starting point for exploring the coastal path to the west, where the views from the top of the cliffs are very fine. It is 1½ miles to the beach at Grève de Lecq and the parish boundary with St Ouen. At about the halfway

BELOW *A beautiful restaurant overlooking Grève de Lecq. Bergerac is just about to stand up the unfortunate Susan and so ruin yet another promising evening.*

BELOW RIGHT *Ship's graveyard – this picture illustrates the dangers of this stretch of the coast. There is very little boating in the area and, unlike the rest of the island, few fortifications, so inhospitable are both the waters and shore.*

point is the fascinating Ile Agois, an islet where Neolithic hut circles have been traced, together with pottery, flint arrowheads and later remains which suggest it was again occupied in the 9th century AD, perhaps by Christian hermits.

Thermally insulated visitors from the 20th century boggle at the idea that anyone should choose this tiny, isolated and windblown spot to make their home, but the fact is that they did, and were not alone in their choice. On both sides of the Channel, from Brittany to my native Cornwall, groups of prehistoric people built cliff-castles and promontory forts in the most inhospitable sites, evidently thinking it was better to be cramped and difficult to attack than to live in more spacious surroundings and risk being overrun and slaughtered by the mob from over the hill.

The Ile Agois is accessible at low tide if you are prepared to climb down the 250-ft cliff, cross the beach and scale the south-west face of the islet. Do not attempt this after rain because the bed of a nearby stream makes the path to the beach highly treacherous; and take great care at all times.

Out to sea is a broad low ridge which might be an island, but is not: Paternoster Rocks. In medieval times it was known as the Pierres de Lecq, then in 1565 Hélier de Carteret, Seigneur of St Ouen, received the right to colonise the island of Sark which lies some fourteen miles off the north-west coast of Jersey.

The island had become a pirate's nest, and to drive them out it was proposed to establish forty families on Sark, each with their own plot of land. Hélier de Carteret chose thirty-five families from Jersey and five from Guernsey. On the journey across to Sark, one of the ships struck the Pierres de Lecq and sank. Several young children were among the victims drowned, and they say you can still hear their cries when a storm is in the air. After the disaster, local sailors and fishermen took to saying an 'Our Father' ('Pater Noster') whenever they sailed near the rocks; in time the word Paternoster was applied to the rocks themselves.

On the other side of Devil's Hole, the eastern boundary of the parish more or less follows the line of the Mourier Valley to the sea. This wooded valley is a little melancholy, becoming prettier as you move further inland, past small farms and cottages where the stream once turned three water-mills. Ducks wander across the narrow winding road, the stream trickles along and, in the gentle sunlight which filters through the trees, there is an atmosphere of fairytale calm; a Grimm Brothers setting, with no violent action to follow.

The stream remains a gurgling brook – the only sound you hear – until, about a hundred yards from the cliff, it turns sharply through a natural hairpin in the rocks; its pace quickens and it broadens to four or five feet in the widest places, falling more steeply. At the cliff edge it cascades over the top and drops thirty feet into the side of a small inlet. At the back of the inlet, beneath the cliff, a tiny beach is paved with enormous smooth elliptical stones, white as sugared almonds.

The Parish Church of St Mary stands almost a mile from the sea, a simple pebbledashed building, politely surrounded but not jostled by a small gathering of houses. St Mary of the Burnt Monastery is the name by which William the Conqueror, then Duke of Normandy, referred to it in 1042 when he awarded it to the Abbey of Cerisy in Normandy along with its lands, one-third of its wheat tithes, and its advowsons (the right to appoint a nominee priest to the benefice).

No-one disputes that there was a monastery here, which was burnt down, but there is little to indicate where it actually stood. Most written sources assume it was near, if not on, the site of the present church. This was itself a modest building at first and stood where the Lady Chapel now is. An interesting medieval relic is the incised stone of Mont Mado granite (from the neighbouring parish of St John) which now lies on its side near the west door, built into the fabric of the church. The incisions depict a man holding a chalice and a fish, the earliest symbol of Christianity, and it is very likely the tombstone of a priest.

The stone probably dates from the time of the original monastery and was rescued and re-used when the parish church was built. This is something of a Jersey habit, for it is not all that unusual to find ecclesiastical relics, such as a piscina where the priest washed the holy vessels during Communion, now walled into an old farmhouse.

Rectors of St Mary's suffered long torment from a noisy custom which had grown up during Jersey's Calvinist period, which itself began in the 1560s and lasted for roughly two hundred years. This was the custom of ringing the church bell at Christmas for 24 hours without stopping. There were no Christmas services in Calvinist times, but once the way was clear to resume having them the rectors of St Mary's came up against the lads of the parish. These rustics, meanwhile, had grown too fond of another tradition, the perk of having a barrel of cider in the church while they rang the bell. In time the perk became more important than the ritual itself, and they were horrified when it was put to them that they should stop numbing their brains with drink while waiting for another turn on the end of the bell-rope.

Rectors who tried to silence the bell, even for the duration of a Christmas service, were manhandled and even beaten up, and any attempt to lock the lads out received very swift treatment – they took the door off its hinges, rolled up another cider barrel and moved into the church. Without the locals' co-operation there was little or nothing a rector could do. The bell-rope dangled next to the pulpit and he had no hope of holding a service while the incessant dong-dong continued. Appeals to the police brought no joy; they wouldn't touch the case.

A turning point came in 1858 when a new young rector went further than others before him. He not only changed the locks, he removed and hid the bell-rope, the clapper and the ladder going up to the belfry. This sent the locals purple with rage. They got out a handbill and delivered copies all round the parish.

Enfants de Ste Marie
Vos droits sont envahis!

Children of St Mary, your rights are invaded! Then they went into action. They broke into the church, fetched a ladder and climbed up to the bell, roused the blacksmith and set him to work forging a new clapper. In no time at all the authority of the rector was turned on its head, and the all-ringing, all-drinking Christmas celebrations resumed for many more years.

All is much quieter nowadays in the village beside the church. If you drive across the top of the island, from Trinity to St Ouen or vice versa, the road takes you past a shining white landmark, the ECOLE ELEMENTAIRE at St Mary's, as the fascia lettering boldly proclaims, with separate entrances for FILLES and GARÇONS.

Lindsay Heath (above), the little scrap that she was when she first played Bergerac's daughter Kim and (left) the promising young adult actress that she has now become.

In the very first episode of *Bergerac*, this was the school to which he came to pick up his little girl, played by Lindsay Heath. She was about three foot six at the time, but that was seven years ago and she has soared since then.

St Mary's is one of the smaller parishes and has the lowest population of any. It is a remote area, most noted at one time for the sheep it bred to supply wool for the island's knitting industry. Perhaps it was by virtue of its solitude and lack of traffic that St Mary's was chosen to stage some of the 'car chases' in *Bergerac*.

I put the term in quotation marks because in an island like Jersey you can't really have them. Not only are there few spots on the island where one car may safely overtake another – except on coastal strips like Five Mile Road in St Ouen and near St Helier – but the terrain itself poses considerable obstacles.

In St Mary's parish, the road network is dominated by narrow country lanes boxed in by high hedges, rather like those in Cornwall and South Devon. The hedges were put there to keep the wind off the fields, and for motorists too they are a most efficient form of obstruction.

Now consider the shape of the Bergerac car, that lovely long-bonneted Triumph Roadster, ancestor of the TR-6 and -7 series. At most cross-roads in Jersey any driver, however carefully he noses forward, must eventually commit himself to a half-second or so of totally blind action, exposing both self and vehicle to heaven-knows-what chances of a meaty broadside collision before he has cleared the intersection, if going ahead, or made his turn and merged with the cross-stream of traffic.

With the Bergerac car all this is true by a factor of about four or five. The bonnet of the Triumph literally hangs out there in Cannonball Alley for two full seconds or so before the driver has a dog's chance of seeing down the road to right or left.

There are, in fact, few cars less suited to the roads of Jersey than Bergerac's Triumph Roadster. We who work on the series are inclined to be philosophical about this. We, after all, remember Bergerac's first car. This was an even more unsuitable vehicle, older, much slower, and mechanically unsound.

On good days the old car could manage a top speed of 20 mph, and we maintained the fiction that it could keep up with anything it chased by undercranking the camera. By this process, taking fewer frames per second, it looked as if the car was going a lot faster than it was. We also had to counterfeit the noise it made. It was not only horribly noisy, with a natural voice like a VW Beetle which has shed its exhaust box, but at no volume, however reduced, did this noise accord with the image of a fallible but generally efficient detective sergeant working for the Bureau des Etrangers. The solution was to lay a separate soundtrack for the car, in which it made the kind of snappy, fast-moving noises you associate with an altogether more rapid vehicle, an MG in good nick, or some such.

The old car also had a basic design fault. It would not stop when you wanted it to. Precisely why this should have been so I am no longer sure, something to do with a dodgy push-rod system, I believe, but the effect was more than once nearly fatal.

Terence Alexander, Debbie Grant and myself in an early photocall on the beach at St Brelade with the first Triumph Roadster. You can tell it is a publicity shot because we are all smiling as though we like each other; true enough, but in the series it was usually a rather different story.

The first time I took it out I almost knocked a small boy down because I could not stop the wretched thing. For another scene I drove up to the gates of a house which that day was serving as the headquarters for a gang of villains. I was to stop, have a brief chat with the guard on duty and then drive through the gates. Came the moment, I approached the guard, he put up his hand and motioned me to stop. I failed to stop, because the car would not, and was on the brink of driving straight through the man when he leapt out of the way quicker than I have ever seen an actor move. Thank goodness he did!

All that, happily, is in the past. We now have the present car which, long-nosed though it may be, is probably sound enough to outlive the series – and some of the cast, too, I shouldn't wonder!

The present Triumph is more resilient, and robust enough to carry a side-mounted camera. In narrow Jersey roads such additional width is extremely hazardous and as the cameras are rather expensive this type of filming is kept to a minimum.

St Mary's parish still has several thriving farms, the farmhouses built of stone in the old style, some with a round-arched gateway to the main yard. Just off the road between St Mary's Church and Devil's Hole is a farm where they are no longer in the business of growing potatoes or raising sheep or Jersey cows. This is La Mare, where Jersey's wine comes from.

The vineyards were planted by Robert Blayney, formerly a wine merchant in the north-east of England and a liveryman of the Vintners Company. He and his wife Ann settled here in 1968, began planting the vineyards a couple of years later and they now have 5½ acres under cultivation (that's 13.2 vergees by Jersey measurement).

In a good year they can produce 15,000 bottles of soft, dry white wine, and they sell the lot, nearly all of it in Jersey with a small quantity exported to the mainland. In a bad year, though, it's another story. The heavy rain and sunless weeks of 1987 brought them down to 2,000 bottles.

'Lots of people tell me that wine-making is a glorious business,' said Mr Blayney one raw afternoon in February as a flurry of sleet turned into a snow shower outside.

'But they tend to be the same people who portray Jersey as an idyllic, permanently warm, balmy, sun-kissed land.'

He has no regrets about his venture, which has grown much bigger and more rapidly than he had ever thought possible, but he is under no illusion that starting a vineyard from scratch is hard work. 'When we started, we had no-one over the garden wall to look at and check what we were doing, and progress was gradual. There were knockbacks too. The farmer next door sprayed weedkiller on his crops, and this blew across to us and set back one part of our vineyard for three years.'

The Blayneys also enjoyed the rare experience of buying and moving into an 18th-century Jersey farmhouse which had never been on the market before, having

Another dry night for Bergerac.

remained in the same family all those years. An old house with such a history does not have to be a wreck, but this one was. Undergrowth ran up to the walls and the previous occupants practised a waste-disposal system which had a medieval flavour to it: containers, peelings, egg-shells, all went the same way – straight out the kitchen door, where chickens, ducks and pigs took what they wanted and left the rest; and there it remained.

As the Blayneys later heard, the pigs were especially assertive and liable to push the back door open when hungry and browse through the kitchen, helping themselves. It

Three coastal scenes.
TOP *St Brelade's Bay looking towards St Brelade's Church and (above) off the east coast.*
RIGHT *Me and Alice in an unusually restrained pose at Corbière point.*

OVERLEAF *Corbière lighthouse set on the shark-teeth rocks, graveyard to a hundred ships.*

The wild and rocky islets to the south of Jersey called Les Minquiers. They boast a helicopter pad (right of the top picture) and a pub – snug under the roof of the first building on the right of the facing page.

FACING PAGE *A remarkably clean Roadster on the causeway to Corbière lighthouse. Alice is off exploring a rock pool. The dangerous rocks are completely covered at high tide as indeed they are about Seymour Tower (above). The seas run fast and dangerously all round this island.*
LEFT *A foaming sea bursts through The Devil's Hole.*

*After dinner stroll in the balmy
Jersey night and (below) Rozel in
the still morning.*

was even rumoured that one particular pig had taught itself to walk upstairs and wake the old man!

'Fortunately, we were not required to inherit the animals,' said Mr Blayney, 'but we did inherit the smell. Wow! It was the most atrocious smell. It was embedded in the ground and we couldn't shift it. No matter what we put down, the smell came back, especially after rain which lifted the stench of pig out of the earth. It was a couple of years before we got rid of it.

'The architects were appalled. To us the house had a certain extra appeal because we were buying something original which had never had the hand of Restoring Man on it. The architects didn't quite see it that way, and refused to let any of their men go in until the whole place had been fumigated. We bought a load of stuff which looked like shredded paper, put it in buckets all round the house, from top to bottom, lit it, and, when it was smoking, retired outside. Smoke came pouring out everywhere, even through the tiles, and at one point we were convinced we had set fire to the place.'

Their perseverance has gained for the Blayneys a marvellous Jersey farmhouse, with outbuildings where they make the wine and also run smaller sidelines in apple wine, marmalades, preserves and mustards. As for the wine, *Clos de la Mare*, it has a little way to go yet before it equals the fruitiness and fragrance of the home-grown Alsace-Rhein wines which are produced from similar grapes. 'We need more sun,' says the owner. 'We are sitting in a low spot at the moment. We are looking for more good summers to give us more wine.'

Sergeant Bergerac, given his unfortunate past, is unable to make an up-to-date comment about this. I, John Nettles, on the other hand, am not averse to the idea of seeing the sun smile brightly on our Jersey vineyard. It's the only one we've got.

Cider Drinkers

ST JOHN

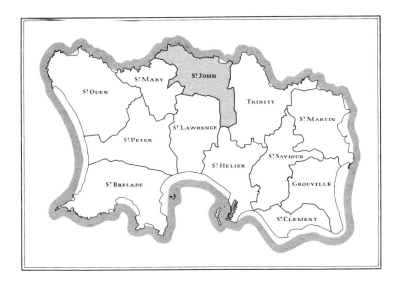

To understand the ways of this mysterious parish, it helps if you are willing to believe in fairies, haunted houses, white stallions that turn into rocks, and a web of other superstitions and near-magic. Every time you turn a corner, it seems, you come upon some unexplained oddity, some stranded fragment of the past.

In St John's you stand more chance of hearing French spoken, or the Jersiais dialect, than anywhere else on the island. And among French-speakers you find a greater adherence to the old beliefs, an appetite for mystery. In times past, when Breton labourers came over in large numbers for the potato digging – and were paid in an old-fashioned combination of cash, cider and a place to sleep – they brought with them the best business of the year for the island's quacks and charmers. These were people brought up to take their ailments to a sorcerer rather than a doctor, and something of this supernatural atmosphere still hangs over the parish, especially around Bonne Nuit Bay.

It is an extraordinarily small and empty place when the summer visitors have gone. Fierce winds hurl spray onto the promenade or, worse still, blow clouds of sand at the unwary walker; when it hits you, it feels like being hosed down with granite chippings, which is exactly what they are.

A single harbour wall, some fishermen's huts, summer shacks for ice cream and teas, a few houses on the road down to the harbour, a hotel on the cliff halfway round the bay, an old fort on the far side. That's all, the rest is granite: granite sand, granite rocks and granite cliffs, rising to 400 feet at La Tête de Frémont on the west side. At face value, Bonne Nuit Bay does not amount to much; and yet it is a small cauldron of romance and mystery.

First the name. Why Good Night Bay? The daftest explanation is that when Charles II, then Prince of Wales, escaped to France from here during the Civil War, he turned and said, 'Bonne Nuit, Belle Jersey.' (Waving, no doubt, an enormous chiffon scarf and dabbing at the corner of one eye.) A more credible reason is that in the 12th century a chapel existed in the parish which was variously called Ste Marie or *de Bona Nocte* (Latin for Bonne Nuit), and later a priory of the same name appears in the island records.

In the middle of the bay is a rock, now known as the Cheval Rock and previously as Le Cheval Guillaume (William's horse). The earlier name reflects the legendary belief that it is not a rock at all, but a magical white stallion belonging to one Guillaume, boyfriend and lover of Anne-Marie, pick of the local maidens.

To give a brief summary of the plot: A wicked kelpie, or water spirit, seeks a human bride. When the beautiful Anne-Marie comes down to the shore one night during the full moon, the kelpie assumes the form of her soldier-lover Guillaume who is away at the wars. She runs to him and he clasps her, and almost drags her beneath the waves to a marriage-bed of seaweed; she is saved only by the arrival of daylight, when the kelpie loses his magic power. Guillaume returns on leave; the day before he is due to go back to war, he finds a magnificent, pure-white stallion in his stable. Next day he is

cantering along the beach on his new charger when it swerves into the waves and threatens to pull him under. Forewarned of danger by a dream, Guillaume has armed himself with a sprig of mistletoe. As soon as he touches the stallion with it, the animal gives out a great shriek, then stiffens and turns into rock.

No more is heard of Guillaume or Anne-Marie, so perhaps they found another horse and just rode off into the sunset. The rock itself became a symbol of good fortune. On Midsummer's Day, which is also the day of St John the Baptist, people came from all over the island to be rowed once round the rock, believing that this would ward off bad luck for one year. Bonfires were lit along the bay and there was much cider-drinking and revelry.

The ubiquitous holiday architecture beside the quay in Bonne Nuit Bay.

Then in 1792 Philippe Dumaresq, publisher of *The Gazette*, came to live in the parish. He decided to enlarge this midsummer rite and set up a two-day fair, with tents selling cakes and clothing, a market for cattle, horses and pigs, an ox-roasting, actors and tight-rope performers imported from France, and a firework display for the finale. These jolly occasions lasted for five years but then the States banned them for being 'contrary to good morals'.

La Crête Fort, built on the east side of the bay in 1835, was one of the last of a series of measures to fortify Bonne Nuit Bay against enemy attempts to land there. Cannons were already installed, a guard house and a powder magazine. Smugglers nevertheless found it an ideal spot for landing and loading goods, and in 1836 the Master of the *Eliza* described one enterprise as follows:

'Instead of proceeding to St Germain, for which we had cleared, we went to Bonne Nuit, and took in 2½ tons of tobacco, spirits in casks, segars, and snuff, which I agreed to take to Wales at the rate of £50 per ton. We proceeded to Fishguard, where we arrived on the fifth day, and, running in about eleven that evening, assisted in conveying the goods to a store close by. We then went to St Germain, took in 32 sheep, and returned to Jersey.'

This account was, according to one source, the Master's *confession*, so presumably his smuggling career was in some jeopardy at the time. Others were happy to carry on the tradition, however, and it is said that a house still stands above the bay which was financed by smuggling profits.

St John's was the biggest sheep-breeding area in the island, and it is appropriate that, on the heights overlooking Bonne Nuit Bay, there was once a Chapel of St Blaize. He is the patron saint of weavers and wool-combers, and these 18th-century Yorkshire verses salute his memory:

Then let us not forget the good,
   The worthy Bishop Blaize,
Who came from Jersey here to us
   As ancient history says.

He taught us how to comb our wool,
   The source of all our wealth.
Then let us still remember him
   While we have life and health.

Quite how the saint had benefited the Yorkshire clothworkers for whom these verses were written is not clear, but we can imagine that they acquired some piece of wool-combing technique from Jersey and were grateful for that. Knitting and weaving were at one time so popular in Jersey that a law was passed forbidding anyone over 15 years old from knitting during the vraicing (seaweed-gathering) season or during seed-time and harvest. The industry continued in the island long after the Chapel of St Blaize was demolished and a house built on the site in 1771.

A more recent sign of changing times is the disappearance of granite from Mont Mado. At one time this hill, less than half a mile from Bonne Nuit Bay, was the source of the finest granite in Jersey, used for facing all the big houses. The States even made it a special requirement that their new buildings should be made of Mont Mado granite. In due course, demand for the stone whittled the hill flat, and then extraction continued below-ground in an ever-deepening chasm. In a book published in 1951, Rev. G. R. Balleine wrote: 'Today the gash is 200 yards broad and about 200 feet deep, and, though innumerable tons of stone have been removed, the supply is far from exhausted.'

The last role for the Jersey tractor is often as a beast of burden on the beach.

If, in 1988, you go looking for Mont Mado granite, even your best map-reading efforts will land you in some agricultural establishment, a farm or nursery yard. 'Yiss, yiss,' cries the man who has immediately come over to see who you are and what you want (they are *very* territorial-minded in Jersey), 'yiss, this is Mont Mado.' And then, after further questioning by you, 'Na, na. The grenit's finish. It's all gone. All pleeowed over.'

It is difficult not to agree with him. All you can see around you is farmland, the road, and a few scattered cottages. You leave. Nowadays, if you want to see granite in the parish of St John's, the place to go is Ronez Point.

This is a slightly weird kind of set-up, not sinister exactly, because all the guys are doing is digging granite out of the cliff, but when you first come upon it, going down the track to Sorel Point, it is like something out of a James Bond movie. One moment all is rustic calm and quiet; to the north-west, the view across the shimmering sea reaches beyond Paternoster Rocks to Sark. Ahead is Sorel Point, topped by a chequered lighthouse and an empty gun emplacement. Then your ear picks up a faint but insistent throbbing, the roar of powerful engines muted by distance. You walk over a faint rise and there, suddenly, all is revealed, just as it is when with one hand Bond parts the elephant grass and Dr No's secret factory leaps into view, the scene filled with uniformed employees going about their business with robotic efficiency, all unaware that a slightly stunned newcomer is observing their every move.

The Ronez company, which owns the headland, has transformed it into a huge granite extraction plant. The pink-brown cliffside is terraced with a great network of roadways leading into the workings at various levels, forming a series of Z-shapes against the cliff; at the face itself, yellow diggers probe and peck at the rock. Heavy trucks and light dumpers move back and forth and the mechanical roaring goes endlessly on, and dust in grey-white clouds sails this way and that across the bay.

An eyesore these quarries may be, but at least they are mercifully concealed from the rest of the island. The twin horns of Sorel and Ronez Points mark the northernmost tip of Jersey, and few people come here casually, unless to walk the cliff paths or admire the views out to sea. Think, too, of all those fine stone Jersey walls, houses, towers, harbours and churches – the stuff had to come from somewhere.

Before we leave, one more piece of mysterious folklore: the Lavoir des Dames. This Washing-place for Ladies is large, rectangular, and sunk directly into the rock next to Sorel Point. Visible at half-tide level, it measures 25 feet by 24 feet and is 15 feet deep. Geologists have long argued whether it is natural or man-made, though commonsense dictates that it must be the result of some freak deposit of soft rock which, initially bedded in the granite, was then worn away and washed out. What ladies, moreover, of ordinary flesh and blood would want a bath of these dimensions, more than twice as deep as a swimming pool, in such a remote spot?

Perhaps they were not ordinary ladies. As ever, the islanders of yore had a supernatural explanation for it. Like so many strange places in the island – the dolmens, hollowed rocks, fountains, etc. – the Lavoir des Dames was, according to them, the work of the Little People (*Les Petits Faîtiaux*) and no doubt was intended to be a bathing-place for fairies. It is also said that if a man saw the fairies bathing there, he would be struck blind immediately. Quite right too.

Alan Lake, a tragic figure, but, when we worked together, a charming companion and an excellent actor. This episode also featured Stephen Yardley, now of Howard's Way fame.

If you head east from here along the Route du Nord for 1½ miles you come to a large car park and pub-restaurant. This is the point of departure for a descent to Wolf's Caves. Some 400 feet down the cliff, reached by a steep pathway followed by 307 steps and a few nifty personal manoeuvres, you come to a 20-foot slash in the granite named after the fossilized wolf and her cubs which, legend has it, were found here. Some spoilsports say this cannot be, and that the name comes from the sea-bass living in the local waters, for which the French name is *loup* or *loup de mer*.

The exploitation of Wolf's Caves was the work of one man, a visionary of the tourist trade far ahead of his time. He was a local landowner and churchwarden, Mr J. H. Pinel, who set to work after hearing the story of Rev. St J. Nicolle, rector of St John's Church from 1891 to 1937, who one day went exploring in the Caves au Loup, as they were then known.

Entering the largest cave from the beach, he decided to settle down and read a book. He failed to notice the tide coming in until it was too late to escape along the beach and up the cliff. He retreated instead to the back of the cave and managed to climb up to a ledge above high-tide level. There, although it was too dark to resume his reading, he waited until the tide came in and had receded, then followed it out through the entrance and walked home.

Mr Pinel was fascinated by the rector's story, which filled his enterprising mind with all sorts of commercial possibilities. His first act was to blast a hole at the back of the cave where the rector had sheltered from the incoming tide, then he rigged up iron ladders, built a zig-zag path with steps where necessary, and opened the site to the public. Near the cliff-top he erected a shack selling soft drinks and tea. It was 3d or 4d to see the caves, and when a party set out for the descent, Mrs Pinel had just enough time to cut sandwiches and make tea before they returned, about twenty minutes later. The shack was later moved to the top of the cliff, was burnt down and replaced by a hotel.

Today the cliffhead establishment is built on ranchhouse lines, the floorspace largely given over to cavernous bars; in one of these, a stuffed wolf in a glass case is the prime exhibit. Appropriately for its shape, the building is also the home of the Marlborough Country Music Club.

Now for a building of another kind. We have filmed in St John's for the *Bergerac* series on more than one occasion. Cécile Paoli and I played some scenes up on Sorel Point, and we also went there with Floella Benjamin, a very sexy lady more widely known for her work in *Play School*. But the scenes that linger most strongly in the memory are from the episode which had the brothel in it.

This is most untypical of St John's parish, I hasten to add, and even of the entire island. I have heard tell, by the way, that there was a bordello in St Aubin during the war, but nobody wishes to spill the beans about precisely where it was located. The locals tend to go 'Hem, hem' and touch the side of their nose with one finger, and no hard information is made available.

Our brothel was located in a very attractive house which had a traditional *tourelle*, or tower enclosing a spiral stone staircase. Inspector Crozier and Sergeant Bergerac, both highly unused to brothel-raiding, burst into the house and were astonished by the range of gear with which our ingenious Props department had equipped the place: a two-way mirror, chains, whips – there was something, it seemed, for everyone. Where they got it all from I prefer not to know. I do remember being impressed by the way these items of sexual furniture contrasted rather oddly with the somewhat ecclesiastical atmosphere of the house itself.

St John's village, surrounding the parish church, is small by comparison with some parish centres though quite a bit larger than neighbouring St Mary's. The Church of St John-in-the-Oak-Wood was one of four chapels in the present parish (those of St Blaize and St Mary (*de Bona Nocte*) have already been mentioned) and by 1150 St John's had become the parish church. It has a pleasant, busy interior, steadily enlarged over the centuries as the population increased, and considerably so at the end of the 15th century when the large south aisle, the tower and spire were built.

A strong sense of community pervades the place. It is symbolised by the custom, maintained to this day, of tolling the church bell at 8 am on the day of a funeral to remind people to put on black. It is tolled once for a man, twice for a woman and three times for a child. In 1979 a new ring of eight bells were cast in the Whitechapel Bell Foundry in London and installed in the church tower beneath the clock. An impressive upright stone inside the church commemorates Abraham De Carteret, Lord of St John, who died in 1681. The bold, deeply incised letters on the stone begin:

Y . SY . GIT . LE . CORPS . DE
(Here lies the body of)
ABRAHAM
DECARTERET
GENTILHOMME
SEIGR DE ST JEAN

People definitely knew who they were in those days.

By some trick of geography, the Centre Stone of Jersey stands in this northern parish, at the foot of a south-eastern pocket which extends halfway down the main road to St Helier. Some guidebooks use a symbol on their maps which means 'worth a detour'; the Centre Stone of Jersey would be lucky to win such an award, but, since few guides to the island seem able to explain exactly where it is or how to get there, let me at least point this out to you.

On the A9, going south, 1½ miles from Haute Croix you come to a village called Sion. Take the turning on the right in the village, which heads north-west; after about 200 yards you pass a gateway on the left, set back from the road and marked Les Chasses. The Centre Stone stands on the ground next to a house wall, close to the road.

A plaque on the wall explains that it was placed there in prehistoric times and is not local stone. It may be part of the lost structure of La Hougue Brune. 'Hougue', by the way, is from the Norse word 'Hougr' and means a mound. Although the Hougue Brune has proved untraceable, others have survived, notably La Hougue Bie in Grouville, probably the most spectacular prehistoric monument in Jersey (see page 100).

The Farmer Dentist

TRINITY

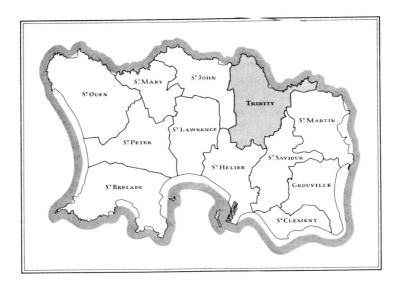

Some years ago, during the shooting of the first series of *Bergerac*, I found myself with the intrepid Inspector Crozier aboard a large tug boat, heaving up and down on a heavy sea just outside the harbour at Bouley Bay. The story required that the Inspector and I dived into the rather forbidding sea in search of some submerged evidence. Neither of us had any experience of diving and it was a little alarming to say the least.

Sean was swept away from the tug by the current and had to be lifted from the sea rather rapidly, and I had similar luck. Gazing at the ship's propellers through the murky, freezing water I thought to myself that I was very probably in the wrong profession. Where were the fast cars, the glamorous girls and the jet-setting life I had fondly imagined to be part of the mini TV star's lot? Not to be found in Bouley Bay, it would appear. I managed to surface to deliver my line to camera and got a wave in the face for my pains. One good thing however did emerge from that rather untoward experience, for I determined to learn how to dive properly so I would never again find myself in such a predicament. The working of sod's law has meant that I have never been called upon to do any serious diving again in the series. But nevertheless the learning and the practice of diving have subsequently provided me with endless hours of pleasure in the warm waters of the Barrier Reef and the even more beautiful seas of the Seychelles. I learned to dive as many islanders do with the famous Jersey dive master Jimmy Webb, a quietly cheery fellow, with, it is rumoured, a colourful background in the circus. It was this same Jimmy who achieved the extraordinary feat of stopping Stan Boardman's endless flow of jokes by introducing him to the mysteries of sub-aqua. You will readily appreciate, dear reader, that conversation is somewhat limited with a regulator stuck in your mouth!

Bouley Bay is where I, along with many others first tasted the delights and occasional terrors of swimming underwater, and hugely exciting it was though it must be said that the visibility is seldom very good and the tide runs very quickly indeed so that great care is needed: but with perseverance great enjoyment can be had from the experience particularly on a summer's day with a full tide when the exotic fronds of seaweed stand in the water like forests.

It is said, though of course I would not know if it is true, that there are scallops to be had a little out to sea when the authorities have their backs turned; if you get caught removing the precious seafood illegally you can be fined, your equipment confiscated for a time and the catch given to the charitable institution, The Little Sisters of the Poor in St Helier – draconian punishment indeed. Bouley Bay is a charming little place with not much parking space but a splendid hotel looking out from its curved frontage toward the distant beaches of France. In the middle of the last century it was proposed as a potential site for the new harbour but St Catherine's was chosen instead (see page 83) and a very good thing too! Up from the little harbour is a steep and twisting hill used by motor enthusiasts to run hill climb races on certain days in summer, much to the chagrin of a least one resident, a Mr Whicker, who lives within earshot of the cacophonous goings on. One may sympathise for the isle is full of noises and sounds,

Looking west around Bouley Bay.

but not always 'sweet airs that give delight'. In high summer the little island roads can be filled to overflowing with thousands of cars and hundreds of coaches and while one sees some of the benefits it does seem a little perverse to deliberately add to the racket which despoils the Jersey summer.

Jersey was occupied by the French for a short period in the 15th century and the countryside to the east was plagued by the Norman *moutonniers* who roamed on horseback stealing the sheep from the Jersey farmers. Philip Ahier in *Jersey Sea Stories* records a traditional story of the time that he discovered written up in the *Almanach de la Chronique de Jersey* of 1881. Whether it is true or not is an unanswerable question but we may assume that it might well be, at least in part. There was a lovely custom in the more communally minded island society of earlier times: to spend evenings in each other's homes, going from house to house on successive nights. Some authorities say that this was an excellent expedient for keeping fuel bills low for plainly one house per night is cheaper to heat than twelve. Be that as it probably was, these *assises de veille* as they were known must have been rather splendid social occasions and much gossip and information, argument and joyful exchanges must have filled the long nights illumined by the light from the cresset.

On such a night during this French Occupation a number of neighbours were gathered in a house near Bouley Bay. The master of the house was a rich farmer, Raulin de l'Ecluse, and this particular *assise de veille* was to celebrate the engagement of his only son, likewise named Raulin, to the beautiful Jeanne du Jourdain. They danced and sang and told old tales, played games, quaffing the sweet cider far into the night. Of a sudden came a knocking and a banging on the door and old Raulin went to open it despite his wife's pleas. A huge man thrust himself unceremoniously into the room insulting the old boy, swearing at the company and peremptorily ordering immediate obeisance. At this the younger boy became exceedingly angry and drove the giant Norman *moutonnier*, for such he was, from the house. The strange fierce man left but not before vowing vengeance for the treatment he had received at the hands of these Jersey folk.

At the end of the long convivial night young Raulin accompanied Jeanne to her home. A storm was blowing up as he began the return journey with his dog Fidèle. Oblivious to danger, and lost in thoughts of his lovely wife to be, Raulin was surprised by the giant Norman brigand this time riding at the head of his gang of *moutonniers*. They wounded the dog and took Raulin prisoner to their cave at Bouley Bay, the Creux Bouanne beneath the valley of the Tombelènes. They flung him bound and blindfolded into a corner while they drank prodigious amounts of cider and feasted on their stolen sheep. At the end of the meal they dragged Raulin before them and after a mock trial they pronounced he was to be hanged by the neck like a common criminal until he died. The noose was placed around his neck.

Meantime Fidèle, his dog, though bleeding from his wound had struggled back to the house of Jeanne du Jourdain who, realising from the state of the animal that something was terribly amiss, rushed into the tempestuous night clad only in her shift; she followed Fidèle to the bay and to the cave. She entered fearlessly and saw her lover, the noose about his neck. She flung herself into his arms and begged the drunken brigands that she might die with him to be together in death, but the giant Norman, seeing how beautiful she was laughed out loud and shouted that she was a

TOP LEFT *Anouta Fleurent, who was to be Bergerac's girlfriend in the first series but fell ill. She later appeared as a guest in a subsequent episode. Other lovely ladies from the series: Louise Jameson (top centre), Liza Goddard (top right), Cécile Paoli (above), Debbie Grant (far left) and Celia Imrie (left), now famous for her appearances with Victoria Wood.*

woman fit for a king and far from being killed she would live to pleasure him. Two of his men came to drag her from Raulin but she snatched one of their daggers and tried to keep them at bay. Raulin in an ecstasy of fear freed himself of his bonds and placed himself in front of his loved one. At this the Norman giant stepped up to the unarmed man and stabbed him viciously through the heart. He tumbled to the floor without a sound. Jeanne, perceiving the death of Raulin, flung herself on his killer and with all the power of anger and despair drove her dagger deep into the brigand's throat and he fell mortally wounded by Raulin's side. She then turned and fled the cave and ran towards the sea pursued relentlessly by the *moutonniers*. She climbed up a rock called the Islet and, as her attackers climbed after her, rather than give herself to them she flung herself from its summit into the boiling sea, screaming Raulin's name high above the clamorous storm. Her body and that of her lover were eventually recovered by the grieving families and they were buried together with all due and fitting ceremony. Ever since that terrible night, when the great storms are backing up and the huge waves pound shoreward, it is said that piercing cries and screams of anguish ascend the air from the Tombelènes and the Creux Bouanne and that these are the lamentations of Jeanne's spirit returned to mourn her earthly tragedy.

Some years ago, Detective Sergeant Bergerac found himself embroiled with the Animal Liberation Front who, thinking to save animals from the pain of experimentation, released several monkeys from some fictional laboratories in Jersey, little realising they were infected with a deadly virus. The story concerned the efforts of the Bureau des Etrangers to round up the diseased monkeys before they infected the entire island. The episode was fairly bland, we thought, but the response on its transmission was amazing. Viewers wrote to me complaining that the anti-vivisectionist case had not been represented fairly, with which I agreed, and others wrote saying that in their opinion the programme showed the Animal Lib Movement for what it was: woolly-minded, anthropomorphic and essentially sentimental. No other episode, as far as I can recall, aroused such emotions.

Whatever the rights and wrongs of the vivisection argument there is, at Les Augrès Manor in Trinity, a marvellous celebration of the animal kingdom, the Jersey Wildlife Preservation Trust. It is not, strictly speaking, a zoo in the sense that Chessington or Basildon are zoos. It was the brainchild of the doughty Gerald Durrell who saw a need to protect endangered species by providing them with a sanctuary in which they could safely breed. They could then be reintroduced in viable numbers into their native habitat. The policy has been strikingly successful and has, incidentally, provided many thousands of tourists with unforgettable sights of extremely rare and well-cared-for animals.

By far the most famous denizen of this beautiful park is Jambo, a massive black lowland gorilla who lives in precarious harmony with his wives and many offspring. He became an international celebrity overnight after a young child fell into the gorillas' enclosure and knocked himself unconscious. Jambo mounted guard over the prone figure keeping, it would appear, the more predatory members of his tribe away, and from time to time stroking the little lad in a comforting fashion. The boy was eventually moved to safety but not before pictures of Jambo's kindly behaviour had been flashed around the world.

I do not like seeing animals penned up as they are in some places in mainland Britain. But if, as here, they have to be enclosed for their own preservation, then it could not be done in a more compassionate, knowledgeable and attractive manner.

The Male Voice Choir

ST MARTIN

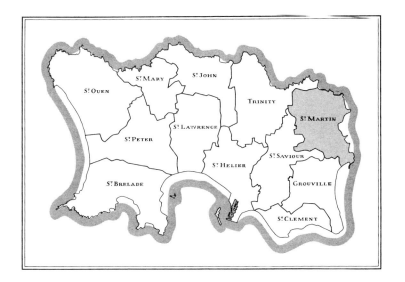

E ast of Trinity, in the north-east corner of the island, lies one of the prettiest of the parishes – a place as different as could be from St Ouen, its counterpart in the north-west. Whereas the latter parish is, in large measure, bleak and wild, bounded by soaring cliffs and wide beaches, St Martin's is ordered, cultivated, neat, a model of island husbandry, and presents an attractive coastline to neighbouring France. It is, moreover, much less overrun with tourists in the summer months.

St Martin's seems to have preserved its essential Jersey quality intact against the ravages of the 20th century. Most of the houses are in the vernacular style, built of local stone, elegant, functional, well spaced and rhyming with the countryside. Here you will find few of the garish piles that litter other parts of the island. The whole effect is one of quiet gentility, permanence, solid tradition and prosperity.

There is, however, one jarring note to be found in the general harmony, the creation of which resulted from a combination of fear and stupidity on an epic scale. As you drive north along the coast road from Gorey towards Archirondel Tower, you will glimpse the monstrosity in question through the trees. It is called

St Catherine's Breakwater, a huge sea wall 826 yards long that points like an accusing finger at the French coastline; aptly so, for it was from fear of French military ambition that it came to be built.

In 1840 the States of Jersey sent a petition to Queen Victoria saying, 'The States . . . have seen with considerable anxiety, the gigantic affairs which have been made on the opposite coast for the enlargement and fortification of the parts of Cherbourg, Granville and St Malo, and on the immense mass of offense which these places will possess in time of war.' They went on to say that Jersey had no large harbour which was not tidal and so no place for warships to have convenient and safe anchorage at all times. In 1846, when relations between France and England had become somewhat less than cordial and Lord Palmerston, he of the Gunboat School of Diplomacy, was Britain's Foreign Minister, the building of St Catherine's Breakwater began. It was the first step in an astonishingly ill-conceived and ill-surveyed scheme to convert the whole of St Catherine's Bay into a huge harbour. Two arms would enclose the inner waters of the bay, one stretching in a straight line south-east from Verclut Point to La Pierre Mouillie and the other reaching out from Archirondel Tower towards it.

Some 70,000 tons of stone were blasted out of Verclut Hill in order to build the massive piers. An army of men were imported from the mainland to work on the project, and the northern breakwater was eventually completed. The southern arm was started, stopped, and finally abandoned in 1856 after building had progressed no more than a few yards. The total cost of the operation was a quarter of a million pounds, and it was all a complete waste.

Why, then, did the British Government pull out after half the work had been done? The reasons offered at the time were richly various: the bay was not deep enough; it contained submerged rocks which should have been blasted but, since they remained, constituted a hazard to shipping; meanwhile, Franco-British relations had improved so much that there was no need for a large naval base. On 11 July 1873, 17 years after the building work had ceased, Lord Halifax gave as the official reason the advance of naval technology: the Royal Navy had begun using steam-propelled warships and these did not have to be protected from the wind as much as the old sail-powered ships of the line. To many contemporary ears this sounded like very convenient reasoning; even today it is hard to look at the huge redundant breakwater without feeling that its construction was underpinned by equally huge acts of stupidity and carelessness by the Government and its agents.

More than a century later the breakwater has served us well on the *Bergerac* series, and so has the old German bunker opposite the nearby lifeboat station. The bunker was dug through the remains of Verclut Hill and after the war was converted by Jersey fishermen into a storage depot for live crabs and lobsters. It now consists of a long tunnel divided in two by a raised wooden walkway, on either side of which are large tanks of salt water containing the crabs and lobsters, which live there for the rest of

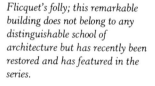

Flicquet's folly; this remarkable building does not belong to any distinguishable school of architecture but has recently been restored and has featured in the series.

Defences old and new.
ABOVE *La Rocco Tower in St Ouen's Bay now restored to its original 19th century splendour and (left) the German observation tower looking out towards Sark at Les Landes.*

OVERLEAF *The venerable Mont Orgueil (Mount Pride) Castle saved for us by Sir Walter Raleigh, who was for a brief period governor of the island.*

TOP *The old (14th century) Grosnez Castle at Les Landes and (above) the fairly old Fliquet Tower.*

RIGHT *The fairly new: a German gun restored and replaced at Noirmont Point looking over Portelet Bay.*

their days with elastic bands around their pincers. In an episode starring Norman Wisdom, Bergerac had to chase a young villain along the walkway, catch him and throw him into one of the tanks. At least, that was what the script said! Unfortunately, I omitted to check the grip of my rubber wellingtons on the wooden surface before filming began. With undue bravado I set off on the chase between the tanks, slipped and fell head over heels into one of them, upsetting the occupants greatly. I suppose being caught and incarcerated with elastic bands around your pincers is bad enough without having an enormous human fall in on you as well! The camera crew enjoyed it hugely; Bergerac was led away by a kindly make-up lady, dazed and bedraggled, his leather coat soaked. A little girl of no more than seven asked me for an autograph as I emerged from the bunker!

Beryl Reid: actrine extraordinaire.

The track up from St Catherine's joins the Fliquet road which runs down past the Martello tower and then turns back on itself by an extraordinary house which looks for all the world like a tiny castle. Close by, in the pleasant little valley, is a rather fine house standing back from the road, owned by some extremely charming and cultivated people who have allowed us to film there a couple of times. On one of these occasions the famous Beryl Reid, noted comic actress and upstager, appeared as one of those demented ladies in which, at least according to the series, Jersey abounds.

Meeting her was rather as I imagine having an audience with the Queen Mother; she was perfectly pleasant but seemed to speak from a lofty remove in in that voice of quiet authoritative control usually reserved for moral lectures to the very young. However, she seemed to enjoy playing her scenes, one of which involved having an hysterical fit, squirming around and throwing herself about on the floor. Now Ms Reid is, it is true to say, of a certain age and it was thought that this would prove a tiring, difficult and fraught scene to shoot; not a bit of it!

I have mentioned elsewhere our cameraman Kevin, or Ripples as he is affectionately known, a youngish Scouser broad of accent and even broader of shoulder, very personable and very good-looking. The day being hot, and the enclosed room in the house made even hotter by our film lights, Kevin elected to wear a T-shirt and a pair of somewhat understated shorts. Ms Reid, from her position on the floor, could make her own appraisal of Kevin's sartorial pretensions as he stood astride her to do the close-ups; and no doubt his enforced proximity increased her appreciation of the ceaseless flow of Liverpudlian wisecracks. For whatever reason, artiste and cameraman struck up an extremely fruitful cameraderie which resulted in a very good scene indeed.

On the far side of St Catherine's Bay, on the way to Gorey, is Anne Port, a charming little cove. There you will find a stone commemorating *Le Saut de Geffrey* or Geoffrey's Leap. Tradition has it that criminals were flung, or forced to leap to their death, from the high rock overlooking Anne Port. Geoffrey, having been convicted of what is coyly described by some sources as a 'crime against a woman', was sentenced to such an end. On the day appointed, a crowd assembled and the prisoner, 'guarded by two halberdiers, was flung into the sea by a masked executioner'.

That was usually the end of the matter, but on this occasion Geoffrey survived his horrendous fall and swam back to land. Half the crowd then wanted the sentence to be carried out again, while the other half said that he should be set free. But Geoffrey, intoxicated by his miraculous escape, settled his own fate by offering to leap again. He did so, smashed against a rock and perished.

There are several variations to this legend, and in the one I like best Geoffrey climbs back to the top of the cliff after his first ordeal and is embraced by a beautiful woman who praises him for his survival. He is so overcome by her loveliness that he declares he will leap again 'pour vos beaux yeux'. However, love at first sight proves no defence against mortality and he dies on the rocks.

The most impressive sight in the whole of Jersey is the castle at Gorey known as Mont Orgueil. It means Mount Pride and the arrogance in its architecture is clear to see. Some kind of fortification has existed here since prehistoric times and the present castle dates from the first decade of the 13th century and was the work of Hasculf de Suligny, then Warden of Jersey. It was built to fend off future attacks by the French and for four centuries it served Jersey well, falling only once, in 1461, to a French force under the command of Jean de Carbonnel. Then for seven years the island suffered a barbarous occupation. Men were abducted and never seen again, women molested and the countryside plagued with bands of mounted Norman brigands, the *moutonniers* we met in the Trinity chapter.

Jersey returned to English rule in 1468 but the days of the castle as the island's first stronghold were numbered. By 1600 it could no longer be defended adequately against a new and more accurate generation of guns ranged on it from nearby St Nicholas Mount, and it was decided to built a more defensible fortress on the small island known as L'Islet near St Helier; thus the present Elizabeth Castle took shape.

Mont Orgueil Castle was saved from falling into disrepair and ruin by Sir Walter Raleigh who became Governor of Jersey in 1600. 'It is a stately fort of great capacity,' he declared, 'both as to maintenance and comfort . . . it were a pity to cast it down having cost her Majesty's father, brother and sister twenty thousand marks to be erected'. The old castle was saved, and we owe a great debt to Raleigh, for Jersey without Mont Orgueil would be like London without its Tower.

Not that the castle enjoyed a quiet retirement in the years after 1600 – far from it. It was the island prison until 1697, prisoners being incarcerated there before being taken to St Helier for trial. During the Civil War (1642–51) many notables of either cause were held there, and an earlier distinguished guest was William Prynne, the puritan agitator, who had his face and ears disfigured for alleged libel and sedition; his three years at Mont Orgueil, from 1637 to 1640, are remembered in the south-west tower named after him.

In World War II the Germans turned the castle into a command and observation post from which they could watch and control the whole length of the eastern seaboard. They augmented their defensive work in Gorey by constructing a huge casemate for a 75 mm gun by the approach road to the harbour. This was mercifully removed in 1972.

Despite its history, its architectural magnificence and evocative atmosphere, Mount Orgueil Castle has figured only once in *Bergerac*. This was in an episode about a German film star (played by Warren Clarke) who was making a movie in Jersey about

A view from the ramparts – Grouville Bay from Mont Orgueil.

Another classic car borrowed from one of the many collectors on the island, in a scene that may have brought back memories of less happy days.

the Occupation. The reason for this lack of coverage is that the castle is so very distinctive. Whereas we have used St Ouen's Manor as, variously, an art gallery, a French château, a gangster's lair and a hospital, and hardly anyone has been the wiser, we could never hope to film the castle at Gorey and expect no-one to recognise it.

If you visit Gorey and the castle there are a number of excellent restaurants to try, including The Moorings, The Seascale and The Galley (according to friends, the last provides the best English breakfast in the island). All these restaurants overlook the harbour, and whenever I eat there a picture of Jimmy Savile comes to mind. We were making a short film for the *Jim'll Fix It* programme, the climax of which took place at the end of the harbour wall. In the script Bergerac has been alerted by a small girl that someone was impersonating Jimmy Savile and conning money from people. Bergerac and small girl then corner felon (Micky Zany) and his accomplice at edge of harbour wall, and small girl pushes both villains off quayside into water. Bergerac then makes unfortunate sexist remark, and he too is pushed into water.

When I volunteered for this watery punishment, the tide was well in. Because of delays during filming, by the time it came to shoot my scene the tide was well out! Consequently, instead of a drop of about six feet I had to fall a good deal farther. I am not good about heights, and when we were ready to shoot the only thing that kept me going was the still greater fear of losing face in front of the BBC camera crew and, of course, the young lady. The moment came, and with a small prayer and a deep breath I plunged off the harbour wall, backwards. I may say that the impact hurt a lot, though not nearly as much as the girl's remark afterwards. I asked her if she enjoyed watching our programme, and she replied that she did not watch it much and anyway it was her mother who had told her to write to Jimmy Savile.

I spend a lot of time in St Martin's parish because the headquarters of the fictional Bureau des Etrangers are to be found there, in an imposing building at La Haute de la Garenne, just west of St Nicholas Mount behind Gorey Castle. It is private property and is very closely marked 'BBC'. Visitors in any numbers are not encouraged for the simple reason that filming would be interrupted by their presence. Nor are coaches allowed along the nearby road, for the very practical reason that the road is too narrow to cater for them adequately.

Pierson House, as Haute de la Garenne has been named, is a very 'institutional'-looking place, and was for many years a home for deprived children. The interior is simple if not spartan and contains the Bureau's offices complete with interview rooms,

Jeffrey's Leap: this time it is supposed to be Peter Jeffrey in for a soaking.

reception area, cells and computers. It is an ideal spot to film for it is set back from the road, it is large enough to cope with generator lorries and caterer's waggons and, above all, it is relatively quiet. This last extremely important for unless you have a quiet ambience you cannot film. However, to find quiet locations in Jersey is difficult. As I have remarked elsewhere, it is a noisy little island particularly in summer when virtually the entire place is on the flight path to the airport, when the whole world and his auntie seem to be waterborne on vessels drive by excessively noisy engines and when, of course, the farmers with their clattering tractors are working all hours to bring in the harvest. For these reasons we are much relieved to be able to film in the controllable environment of the Bureau Headquarters.

Haute de la Garenne is on a beautiful site overlooking the great sweep of the Royal Bay of Grouville, and at the time of writing it is rumoured that when we finally leave the island, it will probably become an hotel. Some enterprising hotelier will then probably call it The Bureau.

I also spend quite a bit of my leisure time in St Martin's, despite it being by Jersey standards an almost unthinkable distance from my home in St Brelade. This is partly because my friends Philip and Jo Forster live in the parish and partly because I have developed a great passion for horse riding. This all began when I had to learn to ride for an episode which involved Liza Goddard – and she happens to be a very good rider.

The Bureau des Etrangers and two of its employees – Peggy, played by Nancy Mansfield (below right), and nicknamed 'Dame Peggy' for her dramatic prowess, and Annette Badland who was Charlotte and went on to situation comedy on television and the stage, and appeared memorably with the Monty Python team in The Holy Grail.

Cynthia Binet, who runs a livery stable above Fliquet Bay called L'Haie Fleurie, bravely undertook to teach me the rudiments. Her family have lived there and thereabouts, it would seem, forever; the accents you hear in the yard are about as Jersey as you will get anywhere and there is always a deal of good-natured bustle and banter about the place. Cynthia's mum, Kate, on one dull afternoon after I had managed to fall off a very ancient and practically comatose mount in the school, cheered me up no end by informing me that she had been over to visit the mainland just the previous week and had discovered, to her surprise, that I was quite popular 'over there' as well, and wasn't that nice to know? Indeed it was.

Ms Binet is a marvellous horsewoman. Astride a horse, she seems hardly to move at all but her mounts do anything she wishes. I on the other hand have to verbally assault, heave on the reins, kick like a fourth-division full-back, to make the haughty beast even acknowledge that I am on its back. At least, that is how it used to be. Now, at last, I have become aware that a horse is not some cleverly designed motorbike to be dominated and driven like a piece of machinery, but rather it is a living being of great subtlety with its own individual rhythms and traits to be understood and controlled so that riding becomes a harmonising of man and beast for the enjoyment of both.

So much for theory. In practice, as one cheeky stable girl remarked, I continue to look like a sack of Jersey Royals when out riding. Ah, but one day . . .

Travelling on horseback is surely the best way to see over your neighbour's wall and to enjoy the Jersey countryside. As I roam about St Martin's I feel rather like William Cobbett on his Rural Rides. A favourite ride is a hack up to the village of St Martin's, and then down through the tracks and lanes towards St Catherine's Breakwater, and up again to L'Haie Fleurie stables. These rides fill me with a soothing impression of control, order and neatness. It is one of Jersey's great attractions that the island is characterised by cleanliness and an absence of disorder, qualities which make it such a pleasant place to live.

Such orderliness is seldom achieved without a degree of compulsion, and Jersey's laws are particularly strict about the upkeep of roads and property. The island operates a system of *Branchage* which makes it imperative for the owners of land adjoining the roads to remove all potential obstructions – overhanging branches, overgrown hedges, fallen stonework, etc. – which might impede the flow of traffic. That people are careful

Charlie Hungerford; gentleman and bonviveur. In his role as Terence Alexander he has been known to enjoy the fine hospitality of the restaurants at Rozel.

to obey these laws derives more, I believe, from a belief in the benefits to be gained from such observance than from fear of the fine that might be imposed for non-compliance – the penalty being 50p.

At the northern tip of the parish lies Rozel Bay, a small popular beach resort with a picturesque harbour built in 1829 as a base for the then flourishing oyster trade. From the Bistro Frère Restaurant high above the bay the visitor may sit at his ease before a glass of his favourite tipple and gaze out across the Channel to France and, before France, the Ecrehous.

The Ecrehous is a reef from which jut several islets, the largest of which are Maître Ile, Marmoutier and Blanche Ile. Ownership of the Ecrehous was long disputed between Britain and France, and only after a ruling in the International Court of Justice at The Hague in 1953 were the islets universally recognised as British. They now also form part of the Parish of St Martin. At The Hague it required 26 public sessions and a mountain of documents going back to medieval times before the Court found in Britain's favour. Ninety years earlier, life was much simpler and the Ecrehous managed very well with their own private king and queen.

Philip Pinel and his wife were crowned in 1863 by the fishing people who lived on the reef in huts and primitive houses. The Pinels ruled for over four decades from a palace/hovel built on the beach of Blanche Ile where large rocks gave them some protection from bad weather though life must have been desperately bleak at times. Philip Pinel crossed over to Jersey about half a dozen times a year to trade batches of the burnt vraic (seaweed fertiliser) which funded his remote existence.

The quality of life on the Ecrehous may be judged from the description of a contemporary observer, P. J. Ouless. 'The only vegetation on Blanche Ile is a few marsh mallow shrubs and some samphire the latter of which when soaked in salted water for a couple of hours and then placed in malt vinegar, makes a healthy and succulent pickle.' After meeting and talking with the Pinels he noted, 'The King told us that he had lived on the "Mainland" when he first came to the Ecrehous. We were rather surprised when he pointed out the Maitre Ile as the "Mainland"; but then everything is relative!'

In 1890 King Philip Pinel sent Queen Victoria a seaweed pannier filled with fish. The Queen responded kindly by presenting Philip with a pipe and a blue coat. In later years, after his wife's death, the King could be found sitting in a tent in St Helier's cattle market where he charged people twopence a time to see his Royal Majesty, wearing his blue coat and smoking his pipe.

Le Couperon

GROUVILLE

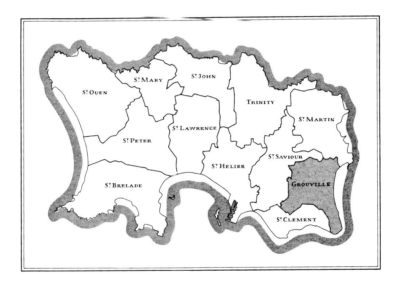

G rouville is a wonderfully varied parish including as it does La Hougue Bie, which alone can justify a visit to Jersey, Queen's Valley, Jim Bergerac's home – a source of endless controversy – the offshore islets known as Les Minquiers, which with the Ecrehous were granted British sovereignty in 1953 by a ruling of The Hague International Court of Justice, and the rock- and sea-girt fortification called Seymour Tower.

This last can be seen about two miles offshore from La Rocque. A large square construction, it was built in the 1780s on the foundations of a much older square tower, following de Rullecourt's abortive attempt at invasion (see page 128). Philip Ahier in *Jersey Sea Stories* suggests that the name L'Avarizon, given to the rocky island on which the tower was built, comes either from the French *avarie*, meaning damage or disaster, with the implication that many wrecks had happened there, or from the word *avalaison* meaning a torrent of water, a probable reference to the speed with which the tide comes rushing in towards the shore. This sudden and frightening threat has had fatal consequences in the past, and I will describe just two incidents.

Ahier supplies the first, the extraordinary tale of four German soldiers who during the Occupation of World War II had walked out to the Seymour Tower and were returning towards La Rocque when

Home from home in Queen's Valley.

the tide turned, rising rapidly and putting them in extreme danger. Their plight was seen by some Jerseymen on the shore who alerted the Germans, and they tried to save their countrymen using an old boat which proved too old and leaky. The sea then remorselessly overtook the hapless soldiers who, seeing no hope of survival, lashed themselves together on a rock, stood rigidly to attention and at the last sank beneath the waves giving a defiant stiff-armed Nazi salute.

A fortunately less tragic event in March 1987 again demonstrated forcefully the speed with which the elements can turn against the unwary in this part of the island. One Saturday afternoon Mrs Rowena Barthorp, an experienced rider from St Martin, and her friend from Dinard, Diana Cumberlege, were out riding their two horses Monty and Dangerman on the beach at Grouville. The weather suddenly took a turn for the worse. At four o'clock, as the tide turned and began its headlong surge across the bay, fog descended and the two riders became completely lost in a matter of minutes. Even though Rowena had ridden on the beach many times before, they found they were riding round in circles. Their own tracks led them twice past Seymour Tower. When they came upon the tower a third time, with the danger increasing all the while, they decided that the only way to save themselves was to ascend the thirty narrow stone steps onto the large platform around the bottom of the tower. The horses went up 'like lambs', as Rowena said, and there they stayed.

Meanwhile Rowena's husband, Captain Raymond Barthorp, had raised the alarm and by six o'clock that evening the honorary police from St Clement had organised a search party and the inshore lifeboat from Grouville was scrambled. One of the officers said that with the weather being so bad, the two women must be 'goners'. Away on the tower Rowena and Diana were thinking on similar lines. Their attempts to get into the tower itself had failed, night had fallen, the tide was rising and waves crashed against the base of the tower, sending up columns of spume to mingle with the dense fog. Rowena Barthorp scratched a message on the wall of the tower with her riding crop. It read, 'Diana and Rowena. So sorry. Please forgive us. Love you all. God save us.'

They fashioned long loops from tackle taken from the horses, tied one end to themselves and the other to spikes set in the wall above their heads, hoping that they might float up with the tide without being washed away. Then they had nothing left to do but wait. They sang hymns together.

They knew that high tide was around 7.30 pm. When that time approached and the water was still some ten feet from the platform, they began at last to hope that they were not going to drown. That hope was shortly given strength when they saw a flare followed by the light of a boat. Ten minutes later a fire service tender, followed closely by St Catherine's lifeboat, came up to the tower. Later that night Diana Cumberlege, suffering from cold and exposure, was taken off. The rescuers forced a way into the tower and there they spent the night, sheltering from the worst of the weather while they waited for low water when the horses could be taken off the tower platform.

Unfortunately, the horses which had so nimbly stepped up the narrow granite steps now refused absolutely to return down them. What was to be done? They thought of bringing a helicopter over from the mainland to lift the horses from the platform, but the fog ruled this out. The next idea was to throw up a great ramp of sand from the beach and lead the horses down it to safety. Yes, it was worth a try. Although not enough diggers could be assembled in time for the next low tide, they could get them for the one after that. Around midnight on Sunday a strange force of three diggers, several tractors and waggons full of volunteers set out from Seymour slip. The ramp had to be built before 4 am on the Monday morning when the tide would once again cut off the tower from the shore. A radio link was established with the shore authorities and the local television company, Channel Television, sent out a generator to light up the tower and help the rescuers to see what they were doing. They finished with an hour to spare. At three o'clock on the Monday morning the ramp was in place and the horses were brought down to the beach.

It is said that once, many years ago, in the Great Marsh in what is now the parish of St Lawrence, there lived a ferocious dragon. For miles around the islanders went in mortal fear of the great beast which wrought havoc wherever it roamed.

News of the dragon travelled across the water to France and a brave and chivalrous knight, the Lord of Hambye, crossed the Channel and engaged the gigantic animal in combat. After a terrible struggle which lasted for three days and nights the good knight finally managed to cut off the dragon's head. However, Hambye's serving man who had accompanied him on his quest, seeing his master weak from loss of blood and the great effort of the fight, murdered him and bore the tale back to France that it was he and not his lord who had slain the dragon. He had killed it as an act of vengeance after the dragon had overcome Hambye.

The servant also claimed that, with his dying voice, his master had wished him to marry the Lady of Hambye, and in due course the innocent lady took the murderous villain as her husband. But 'Murder though it hath no tongue, will speak with most miraculous organ' – and so it was in this case. One night in his sleep the servant babbled of what he had done crying 'Wretch that I am to have murdered my Lord.' His crime was brought to light and he paid for it with his life.

The Lady of Hambye caused a small hillock to be raised over the spot in Jersey where her Lord was interred; above it she ordered a small chapel to be built where prayers could be said in memory of her dead husband. The full name of this monument was said to be La Hougue Hambye (the mound of Hambye), which became abbreviated to La Hougue Bie. The truth is probably more prosaic.

'Hougr' is the Viking word for mound and its original use was much older, although it is likely that the 'Bie' does refer to the Hambye family who flourished in the 12th and 13th centuries in the Cotentin peninsula in France. The mound is one of the finest examples in Western Europe of a Neolithic Passage Grave. Built of 69 huge stones weighing up to 30 tons each, it contained at one time eight bodies including those of three women.

Like another famous tomb of the period to be found in Ireland, it is so built to catch the first rays of the sun rising at the winter solstice. It was excavated in 1924 after the enterprising Société Jersiaise had purchased the site. Just as at St Brelade's Church and the Fisherman's Chapel nearby, this old sacred ground was later used for the construction of Christian places of worship. Apparently there was a chapel at the western end and to the east a living area, presumably for the priests, many decades before Dean Richard Mabon built his distinctive Jerusalem Chapel there in 1520. This cleric had made a pilgrimage to the Holy Land, as was the custom of the time, and on his return built a reconstruction of the Holy Sepulchre in Jerusalem. This was housed in the dome you can see at the eastern end of the mound, and it is said that Mabon used this chapel to perform fake miracles, tricking many gullible people into parting with their money.

We are fortunate that the Société Jersiaise has restored the site, including the passage tomb, to its original splendour for towards the end of the 18th century the site had been despoiled by one James d'Auvergne who had a sham medieval tower built on top of the chapels. This was removed in 1924.

James d'Auvergne bequeathed La Hougue Bie and its tower to his famous nephew, Philippe d'Auvergne. Philippe (1754–1816) was an extraordinary man. Dauvergnes was his real name; a Jerseyman by birth, he was adopted by the eccentric Prince de Bouillon, ruler of a small principality in France to the north-east of Sedan. The family

Having a clear-out with Francine, in a very early episode to judge from the hairstyle.

La Hougue Bie, with the chapel of Notre Dame de la Clarté perched above the distinctive dome which housed Mabon's recreation of the Holy Sepulchre.

name of this Prince was De la Tour d'Auvergne, which Philippe thought similar enough to Dauvergnes to imply a certain kinship, though of course this was challenged in later years. Philippe was thus translated to the ranks of minor royalty and he took his elevation most seriously.

He is nowadays best remembered for his excellent work on behalf of the British Government during the Napoleonic Wars. He cleverly organised a network of spies and secret service agents from among disaffected elements in Normandy and Brittany, those regions being less pro-Napoleon than other parts of France. In this way he gained vital information to send back to the British military commanders. Unfortunately his ambitions to reign as Prince in Bouillon were never realised despite lengthy and expensive legal proceedings. The principality was taken over by the Dutch and Philippe received not a penny in compensation. He went bankrupt and died as such on 18 September 1816. 'Broken hearted, ruined in health and purse, he had no desire to live' – thus the description of a family friend. La Hougue Bie was then sold as part of his estate to satisfy his creditors.

Here I am boring Cécile to death with my one-fingered version of a Russian dance which is the only tune I can play on the guitar. I have since lost the guitar, which my friends say is a blessing. Cécile is making a good pretence at interest but then she is a good actress.

I remember some years ago sitting in the old Triumph one very hot summer day on the road leading to Blanc Moulin Farm, and thinking idly to myself about the beauty and tranquillity of Queen's Valley. I looked across the track to the meadow beyond and through the haze I saw old Marie Travert, dressed in an old-fashioned Jersey bonnet to protect her from the sun and a long black voluminous dress which reached to her ankles. She was leaning against a bale of hay talking to a little calf which had been born a couple of weeks previously. Her voice, unselfconsciously loud, reverberated down the valley filling the air with the strange sounds of Norman French.

Marie Travert had lived in the valley for nearly thirty years with her son Louis. I met her once. She sat in her kitchen, her hands, swollen with years of manual labour, folded quietly in her lap, and spoke in the old Jersey tongue of her sadness at the coming of the reservoir. I followed her as best I could. When in 1976 the news broke that the valley was going to be flooded to make a reservoir she had killed all her hens and chicks, and allowed her small herd of cows to dwindle to just one or two. Those who were close to her say she lost her will to live the day she thought she had lost her home.

Marie Travert died last year, but when we film at the old farm, as we still can because the valley is not yet flooded, I feel sometimes I can see her in the sun-drenched fields and hear her voice echoing up the little valley.

The story of Queen's Valley is very much a story of contemporary Jersey, or how the pressures of so-called progress can change and destroy the shape of the land and the customs of the ages. The valley is now going to be turned into a reservoir to satisfy the ever-increasing demands for water of an ever-increasing island population which rises to more than 120,000 during the summer months. It has taken nevertheless over a decade of debate, demonstration, public inquiry, private inquiry, lobbying, petitioning and litigation finally to reach the point of starting the work. If the debate has done nothing else it has served to make people think about the importance of conservation and what kind of island they want Jersey to be in the years ahead.

The Guthrie Water Enquiry Board, which was set up to produce a report on the whole affair, actually found against the need for a Queen's Valley reservoir and suggested, instead, a system of all-island metering and an investigation into the possibility of an underground reservoir in St Ouen. That was in September 1978. The Public Works Committee then considered the report and set it aside, recommending that the best way of avoiding future water shortages was to build a 250-million gallon reservoir in the Queen's Valley; the States Assembly accepted this decision by 25 votes to 23. This being Jersey, though, the arguing did not stop there and indeed continued unabated until 1988. Legal arguments were deployed to prevent compulsory purchase of the land on which to create the reservoir; David Bellamy, Des Wilson and no less an authority than Gerald Durrell weighed in on the conservationist side. All, finally, to no avail. The tide of opinion in the States was running very much in favour of the reservoir and so it was that in spring 1988 the necessary enabling act was passed by the Queen in Council and building was scheduled to begin soon afterwards.

The loss of the valley has become an unavoidable tragedy. Many people on the island still find it hard to grasp that they will never again be able to see Queen's Valley as George Eliot, Victor Hugo and countless generations of Jersey folk have seen it. But if you chance to pass by on one of the new roads alongside the reservoir, spare a thought for Marie Travert and her home, fathoms deep in the dark water.

Driving Home in the Rain

ST CLEMENT

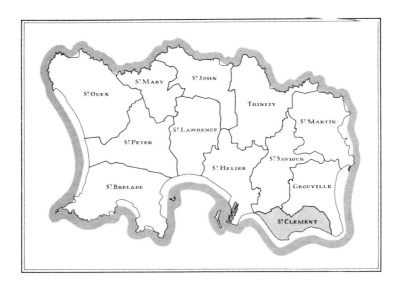

One pleasantly conspicuous trait shared by the inhabitants of this parish, the smallest in Jersey, is that they are very proud to be from it or part of it. As an expression of their local feeling they stage a marvellous annual fête, possibly the best on the island.

Everyone turns out for it and the mood is dependably merry, vibrant, a trifle raucous, very St Clement's. Other parish fêtes have tended over the years to align themselves towards the holidaymaker, so much so that they have all but lost their Jersey identity, but in St Clement's they are wise enough to keep the flavour local.

A somewhat surprising man, and yet an oddly typical native of St Clement's, is Dr David Spencer, the pathologist who advises us in the *Bergerac* series. He is probably

one of the few pathologists who conforms closely to the film idea of what a pathologist should look like. He will not, I hope, mind if I say that at times he can appear quite frightening! A notably large head, with overhanging beetling brows and a rocklike square jaw are impressive physical features which can daunt not just the newcomer, though he is in himself a very gentle man.

In common with others of the medical profession, he possesses a somewhat gory sense of humour. We have filmed at various times in the Pathology Lab. in town and there we found, pinned to the wall, an entire hotel league championship based on the number of guests dying in each place. The establishment with the largest number of deaths in any one year was then declared the winner – and no doubt its progress in the following year's competition was monitored with interest.

In Pathology they have been known to run a Liver of the Year award. This was awarded to the corpse possessing the most enlarged liver as a consequence of its

owner's over-indulgence in alcohol. On an island which suffers from alcohol abuse to an almost alarming extent, some of the finds have been quite startling. They had one liver which had swelled to three times its proper size before its owner was no longer in a position to continue attacking it; being, by then, dead.

Alcohol is nothing new in island life. The whole of Jersey used to be covered in apple orchards to provide the cider which was the main product of the island and, of course, a degree of drunkenness went hand in hand with that – plus ça change.

There is an aptness about Dr Spencer's connection with St Clement's. Few places could be described as having a landscape with pathological characteristics, but there is something so abnormal about the ragged outlines of 'Moonscape Beach' that the link is not inappropriate. What is more, this south-east corner of the island was in centuries past a desolate and sinister spot, a lonely stronghold of morbid, ungodly preoccupations and terrifying commotions in the night.

None of this is evident when you enter St Clement's from its western end. Here the parish is the architectural twin of several Sussex towns-by-the-sea. The modest sand and stone coloured villas which parade along the Grève d'Azette (*grève* means sandy shore) are a 19th-century outgrowth from St Helier and could be substituted overnight for a stretch of road heading into, or out of, somewhere such as Lancing, Littlehampton or West Worthing. Were such a transformation to be carried out, only the most sober Jersey householders would be expected, on waking the next day, to notice that they were in another country. Unless, of course, they looked out to sea.

The view across the bay, looking west, begins promisingly at the far lighthouse on Noirmont Point and the woodlands above Belcroute Bay, then, as the eye moves into St Aubin's Bay, the distant prospect is overlapped by the oil terminal at St Helier and a cluster of horrendously visible storage tanks near the tower of La Collette, then by the

TOP *St Brelade's Church and Fisherman's Chapel and (above) a neolithic passage grave at La Pouquelaye de Faldouet.*

RIGHT *A more extrovert religious house just behind First Tower. The IDC once had the temerity to complain that this was 'unsightly' but island opinion fully supported Mr Bisson's colourful eccentricity and so it remains, though he is fast running out of space for his quotations.*

Four sights of the intensive island husbandry.
ABOVE LEFT *Working the 'cotils' (narrow sloping fields) and (above right) St Helier's utterly delightful Victorian market built in 1882.*
RIGHT *A typical Jersey field of potatoes and (facing page) some fields at L'Etacq wrapped in polythene to protect and force the early crops, seeming to become part of the sea.*

OVERLEAF *Portuguese seasonal workers who form the major part of Jersey's agricultural (and hotel) labour force.*

TOP *A modestly elegant house in a style very popular in the island, but even more typical (right) is this farm in Queen's Valley for long the home of James Bergerac, soon to disappear forever when* the valley is flooded. Note the sleek Jersey cows in the meadow (and above), carefully bred and despite their gentle expressions a remarkably hardy species.

*Valleys, trees and vernacular
architecture to be discovered
along the six hundred miles or so
of inland lanes.*

skyscrapers of Havre des Pas. Above these urban pinnacles the angular undulations of the roof and dome of Fort Regent top the skyline, suggesting a saucer-breasted Picasso woman swimming, elbow bent behind her head, in eternal backstroke towards the sea.

In the peace of a February mid-morning in 1988, an elderly lady arrived on the empty promenade by the sea wall carrying a battered brown shopping bag such as she might have taken with her on a foraging expedition to the Home & Colonial Stores in about 1948. (They say Jersey now lives in the 1950s but sometimes I think that is a bit too recent.) As I watched, she upended the shopping bag with one abrupt movement and tipped a bulky shower of finely ground meal onto the pink stones of the sea wall. Just as suddenly, out of nowhere, more than two hundred yelping shrieking gulls collected in the sky above and began thrashing for airspace as they descended in a ragged umbrella formation. How prudent of her to wear glasses, I thought, as the turmoil of hooked bills and splayed feet suspended from heavy bodies threatened to close over her head.

She was wise to their ways, however, this benefactress of the birds, and nipped sideways a few steps at the very last moment, then watched, head on one side, with nannyish pleasure as her familiars alighted on the sea wall and promenade and quickly ran through the ceremonies of the pecking order.

Half a minute later, the party was over. Leaving a good three-quarters of their elevenses behind them, the gulls lifted off and flapped easily back to the shoreline and the tastier pickings of winkles and other live food to be gleaned from the wet sand. The lady, too, vanished, as quickly as she had arrived. Was she, by great good chance, a locally famous figure, perhaps the Phantom Biscuit Lady of St Clement's? I think not, but four hundred years ago she might have been viewed very differently. In this sparse corner of the island people would certainly have found something to mutter about if an old woman had made a habit of throwing whole bags of precious food to the gulls. Was she in league with them, did she have power over them? 'Not natural, is it?'

Many an unfortunate was accused of witchcraft on far flimsier grounds than consorting with seagulls, and St Clement's in those days was the notorious hub of witches and their black rituals. At Le Nez Point, just around the next headland, stands Rocqueberg, a 40-foot granite rock where witches gathered to dance and raise storms at sea with their singing, summoned there by 'Le Tchéziot', the Devil's deputy and lord of the witches and charmers. The top of the rock, which is now in a private garden, has been vitrified by lightning; halfway down it is a ledge that bears what many believed was the cloven hoof-print of the Devil.

Active witchcraft took various forms. In some it began as a simple rebellion against the repressions of Church law and the narrow-mindedness of family life. Others went beyond a desire to be eccentric, and positively pursued the worship of the Devil. Yet others were white witches, using charms, love philtres and other magic to try and cure their superstitious clients of all manner of physical aches and desires. When devil-worship was rife in Western Europe in the late 16th century, it found many adherents in Jersey and the Courts were grimly unforgiving as they dispatched dozens of witches to the gallows. The traditional sentence was that she should be 'hanged and strangled by the public executioner till death ensues, after that her body to be burned and entirely consumed'. (Not all Jersey witches were women, by the way, though the majority were.)

One of the more famous stories about the witches of Rocqueberg is known as 'The Thirteenth Fish'. All fishermen passing the rock were required, for their own safety, to hand over a tribute or passport to the witches. The thirteenth fish of his catch was the chosen tribute, and the fishermen had to throw it onto the rock to guarantee his safety. Failure to give up his thirteenth fish brought instant punishment: his boat would swing about and head directly for the rock and be smashed to pieces. Some fishermen forgot to pay up, and some with traditional Jersey cunning tried to slide past unobserved, but none escaped the fatal wrath of the witches.

One day, a young fisherman was returning with his catch when he saw the weird sisters on the rock dancing and singing blasphemous songs. A great storm blew up, but the fisherman just laughed to see the witches and looked down at the special tribute he had brought them – an enormous five-armed starfish. As he sailed up to the rock he took his knife and hacked off one of the arms, then he threw the starfish at the witches. The four arms landed on the rock in the form of a cross and at that moment the fisherman shouted:

'La Crouée est mon passeport' (The Cross is my passport).

Immediately, the storm ceased and the witches vanished, and from that day no-one has ever seen a witch at Rocqueberg. Despite their demise, the reputation of St Clement's for sorcery and evil lasted for many more years. In 1875 a local guidebook explained:

'No Jersey girl or Jersey man would have brought you here [Rocqueberg] on a Friday night, particularly if there was a full moon. The Prince of Darkness has a special fancy for the locality. He frequently came here in former days and still manifests himself.'

Aside from its satanic connections, the parish has the most bizarre sea front in Jersey. 'Moonscape Beach', they call it, referring to the rocks which jut from the sea and stand fully revealed when the tide goes out – and here it can go out for two miles. Outcrops of brown rock occur from Grève d'Azette Bay all the way through St Clement's Bay and round the corner into Grouville, wrapping this entire south-east corner of Jersey in a band of raw geology, a giant's maw of broken rock-teeth in which, at low tide, large pools of water lie trapped in the deeper cavities. So strange is the spectacle, it seems an ideal locale for witches and magicians, and indeed this may be why they were drawn to settle in St Clement's.

One of the larger rocks is an islet and once, long ago, was inhabited: Green Island, or La Motte (The Mound), as it was originally known. It is a large grassy-topped slab standing about 200 yards from the sea wall. From the car park at Le Nez Point, walk down the stone-ribbed slipway, across a strip of pale sandy beach and then, if the tide is with you, pick yourself a path across the rocks until, at Green Island, you step, as it were, out of the sea onto the island. This is the largest remaining outpost of an eroded strip of coastline formerly attached to Jersey. To this day the old forest bed lies only a foot or so beneath the sands at Grève d'Azette. Prehistoric burial chambers were found on Green Island in 1911 and the bones and other remains can be inspected at Jersey Museum in Pier Road, St Helier.

If, by the way, you go for a stroll on Moonscape Beach, take care. The tide can turn in ten or twenty minutes and then rushes in at perilous speed. Even between Green Island and the shore you could be in trouble. We have filmed there several times – and a quaintly surreal spectacle we make, by the way, all dressed up to the nines, hair elaborately coiffed, crawling across a clump of rocks in the middle of the ocean; it's like a scene from a space opera. On one of our very first episodes we managed to get ourselves cut off by the tide and had to be brought back in longboats with one Captain Coom in command. The good captain, who looks after the film unit's naval requirements, was clearly more worried than we were, probably because he was aware of the dangers.

Ian Hendry was with us one day on Moonscape Beach. Then suddenly he wasn't. We lost him. It was a cold blustery morning and we stared out at the bleak rocky landscape which seemed to stretch halfway to France. Where the hell was Ian? We looked and looked but no-one had a clue where he was. For the time being, he had disappeared.

'Eee-aaaan!' somebody was calling across St Clement's Bay. 'Where are you?'

'I'm here,' declaimed a Scottish voice suddenly from behind a nearby rock, and then a hand rose into view, clutching a bottle of vodka. Ian had decided to take pity on us.

Filming resumed. Even slightly tipsy, he was a brilliant performer, and his loss is very much lamented.

Other land and sea marks in St Clement's Bay are the Icho Tower, a 28-foot Napoleonic structure built on the islet of Icho which lies a mile and a quarter out to sea; the tower at Le Hocq, halfway round the bay, which was built around 1780 after France had sided with Britain's rebellious American colonies; the tower on the eastern end of the bay at Plat Rocque point, which is just across the parish boundary in

ABOVE LEFT *Ian Hendry: actor.*

ABOVE *Icho Tower, a famous seamark and a welcome sight to many sailors. It is the first sign of home to those approaching from the south.*

Grouville; and the splendidly pugnacious and very filmable Seymour Tower on the islet of L'Avarizon, just over a mile out to sea.

Before we leave the seaside, here is one more spooky tale. It concerns The Bull of St Clement, who once every four or five years raised his head and gave out a prolonged and frightening cavernous bellow which echoed along the shore and, curiously, came from somewhere out to sea. A suitably monstrous legend grew up around this terrible noise, and many in the parish were convinced that a gigantic amphibious bull lived out beyond the rocks, and roamed the reefs of 'Les Grands Houmets' when the tide was exceptionally low.

The Bull roared on until the turn of this century, when a Mr Sinel arrived in the parish and began collecting descriptions of the noise from local people. Deciding it was a lot of nonsense, but unable to say why, Mr Sinel went out sand-eeling on the ebb tide with his son and a Mr Dancaster, together with a boatman. While the others concentrated on searching for eels, Dancaster went off to explore a high ridge of rocks.

The three were still busily fishing when, from almost under their feet, a roar as loud as a hundred bulls boomed through the afternoon air. Then Dancaster's head poked up from behind a boulder. 'Do you want to hear him sing?' he asked his astonished companions.

When the others had climbed over to him, he placed his hand over a small cleft in a rock pool. Immediately the roar, which had been continuous and extremely loud, died back to an echoing wail followed by silence.

The Bull of St Clement was an entirely natural phenomenon which worked like a highly amplified version of water draining from a wash-basin. Beneath a dome-shaped rock, as Dancaster now showed his companions, was a hole half-filled with water. At very low tides, the top of the hole was exposed and a vacuum created as water drained away through it. Such was the rock formation beneath, a kind of echo-chamber was set up which issued the roaring sound which had so terrified the natives for generations.

Thus enlightened, Mr Sinel is reported then to have uttered one of those heroic lines rarely found outside Victorian or Edwardian school stories:

'You'd better plug the pipe, Dancaster,' he ordered, 'and kill the bull.'

This was immediately done, though with hindsight it seems rather a pity. It might have made a wonderful tourist attraction today, and an impressive nature film, too, complete with souvenir audio-cassette. Alas, we shall never know how bull-like the Bull really was.

At the eastern boundary of St Clement and Grouville, take the back road to Fauvic and pass rows of greenhouses where you may see immensely tall tomato plants pressing against the glass. Ahead, a line of côtils (steep fields) are a further reminder of the meticulous industry of the Jersey farmers who cultivate such fields, conquering their almost backward-leaning gradients by dropping a plough down from the top, on a rope. Just along here they have a Heartbreak Road (Rue du Crève Coeur) which climbs straight up the hill; not terrifyingly steep, to start with anyway, but I expect it would get to you if you had to walk it a dozen times a day.

Turn left at Fauvic on the road to St Helier and in a mile or so you come to the parish church. A wooden chapel probably stood here in pre-Norman times, followed by a stone chapel, and the parish Church of St Clement was certainly established by

BATTLE OF JERSEY
JANUARY 6TH 1781
THE FRENCH TROOPS UNDER THE COMMAND
OF BARON DE RULLECOURT
CAME ASHORE HERE

A plaque commemorating the Battle of Jersey sits below a rather interesting house where we have occasionally filmed. We call it the 'Psycho' house for reasons obvious to those who remember that great Hitchcock classic.

1067. It was considerably enlarged in the 15th century, the chancel and transepts being added to give the church its conventional cross shape. In the south transept of this long and simple building is a sturdy font which dates from 1400 and is as fine a piece of sculptured granite as you will find in Jersey. During the Reformation it was thrown out of the church and only uncovered in the 19th century by workmen opening a trench on the north side of the churchyard.

These same men, or perhaps their mates, were responsible for discovering, in 1879, the church's most celebrated treasures, its three frescoes or wall paintings which for centuries had lain hidden beneath layers of plaster. These light and elegant images were painted some time in the 15th century; one tells of St Michael slaying the dragon, another how St Margaret, attacked in prison by the Devil in the shape of a dragon, made the sign of the Cross on his breast which rent him in two and allowed her to escape. Only a fragment remains of the latter, and that is all we can now see of the third fresco which illustrates an old French poem, *The Three Living and the Three Dead*. Though little survives of this medieval work, the visible pieces are very fine, movingly simple and direct.

Continuing towards St Helier along the Grande Route de St Clément, we pass the burial site on Mont Ubé where 28 upright stones mark a passage grave. These, too, like the font buried in the churchyard, had suffered badly from neglect and in the early part of the 19th century were serving as a pig-sty.

Nearby is Samarès Manor, a 'power house' of the past which still exudes a feeling of wealth and position. Set back in spacious grounds, the two-storey manor house is not spectacularly large but the long banks of rhododendrons which flank it, the working farmyard on the east side, the herb gardens to the west, the lake and fishponds all contribute to a certain quiet grandeur. The *colombier*, or dovecote, facing the front of the house, is a fine specimen, thought to be the oldest in Jersey; the interior of the 20-foot circular tower is pierced with 17 tiers of nesting places, now empty save for the odd empty crisp packet and other random deposits from the tourist trade.

Large areas of this parish lie below the highest tide levels, and before the States built a sea wall in 1811, following the worst flooding of all, the sea not infrequently broke through, submerging fields and washing entire roads away. The country to the south of the manor house was a salt marsh, and if you tinker somewhat with the word 'Samarès' you end up with a run-together version of the Old French *salse marais*, meaning a salt-water marsh. Here in Norman times salt was collected by letting the sea run across the land, then sealing the access channel and leaving the water to evaporate from the salt accumulated beneath.

The Seigneurs of Samarès, or lords of the manor, were powerful men indeed, running their lands according to feudal laws and customs which put them almost on a par with royalty. The bodies of local criminals and other sinful tenants, including witches, swung from the lord's private gallows; he claimed shipwrecks, kept a rabbit warren, hawked and hunted with dogs and ferrets on lands extending as far as Fort Regent, and made sure that his tenants were kept in their place. They, meanwhile, had to do many things for their Seigneur (or else!) in addition to farming their own patch – make his hay, fetch his wood and wine, clean out his *colombier* whenever necessary and, once in each tenant's lifetime, transport him across the sea to one of four Norman ports. The rector of St Clement's also had a special duty to perform: whenever the lady of the manor had a baby while in residence in Le Homet fief, the rector was obliged to supply a white horse to carry her to church for a Service of Thanksgiving, to be held on the day she rose from childbed.

Various families have held the manor since Norman times – de St Hilaire, de Saumarèz (a junior branch of the de St Hilaires which took the name of the manor for its own), Payn, Dumaresq, Seale, Hammond, Mourant, Knott. Sir James Knott, who bought the property in 1924, spent immense sums to drain the marshes and create the splendid gardens which are now the great pride of the place. At one time Sir James employed forty gardeners and scouted far and wide for exotic plants, some of which can still be seen where he placed them: the Metasequoia or water larch from Central China, the Ginkgo or maidenhair tree from Eastern China and the Tulip tree from North America. Do not miss, though you are unlikely to, the walled herb garden where more than a hundred species of herb grow in four plots - culinary, fragrant, medicinal, and cosmetic and dyeing.

There had been a keen gardener at Samarès three centuries before Sir James, when Philippe Dumaresq, a friend of the diarist John Evelyn, was in charge. He dug a canal a quarter of a mile long to drain the grounds, planted cypresses from France and founded a vineyard. He it also was who, in 1678, for defence reasons, transferred Town Hill, which was part of his fief, to the Vingtaine de la Ville. This made it possible for a fort to be built there should relations with France grow any worse. The Dutch War was raging and Louis XIV had mustered a fleet of some size at St Malo. Invasion was feared but did not come about, and it was more than a century before the first stones of Fort Regent were laid.

If, on leaving St Clement's, you head west towards the town, your route may take you through the tunnel beneath the Fort. Spare a thought, as you enter, for the Lords of Samarès and their retainers who once chased in glorious freedom over those hills with their dogs, nets and hunting poles. Those, surely, were the days – if you were rich.

The Jersey Farmer

ST SAVIOUR

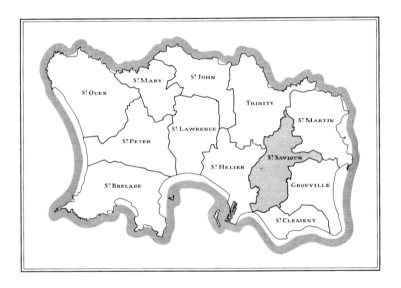

Much of the western part of this parish has had to absorb various waves of overspill from St Helier, with unattractive results. A journalist on the *Independent* newspaper, in a rather scathing article, suggested that the only joy to be had in Jersey was to observe what he called the 'Torbay mentality' in action, all pebbledash fancy porches and plastic gnomes.

He must have been feeling depressed if he allowed a few acres of suburban sprawl to blight his overview of the island. One of the great things about Jersey is that it takes so little time to move on to the next place, which you can reasonably hope will be an improvement. In St Saviour's one of the two main escape routes from the east side of St Helier takes you along the Grouville road (A3) to Longueville Manor, an excellent place to restore the spirits. As manor houses go, it is a fairly unpretentious building; now a hotel, it contains a splendid if expensive restaurant, but I would like here to draw your attention to the magnificent arch at the main entrance.

Arches figure often in traditional Jersey architecture, there being several categories and many variations within each of these. The arch at Longueville is described by Joan Stevens in her classic work *Old Jersey Houses (Vol 1)*

as 'one of the oldest as well as the largest and most ornamental of all round arches in the island and one which can be very closely dated. It has three concentric chamfers [concave edging] and is surmounted with the arms of Hostes Nicolle who was Bailiff from 1560–64.'

The Bailiff Hostes Nicolle was of Cornish stock and bought Longueville Manor in 1480. What little we know of him is not pleasant and derives from this account in the *Chroniques de Jersey* (1585). 'There was a poor man whose house adjoined that of the Bailiff. This land the Bailiff coveted. So one day he bade his servants kill two of his finest sheep and carry them to the house of a man who was by trade a butcher. He then roused the Constable and his officers and bade them search the butcher's house where they found the sheep hanging in his stable. The man was brought into Court and condemned to be hanged that day. As the hangman put the rope round his neck at the door of the Court, the poor man said to the Bailiff, "I summon you to appear within forty days before the just Judge of all to answer for this!" And on the 39th day Nicolle fell dead by the wayside as he was returning from town.'

The Manor also boasts a *colombier*, or dovecote, possession of which was the privilege of a Seigneur of a fief. They represent a primitive form of battery farming, their purpose being to provide people with the wherewithal to make pigeon pies during the lean winter months when other food could be in very short supply. The *colombiers* in Jersey are quite large and accommodated up to 1,000 birds. Most are

circular in shape though there is a square one, rebuilt in 1647, at Hamptonne which is at the head of Waterworks Valley in St Lawrence. Among the better preserved examples are those at Samarès Manor in St Clement's and Rozel Manor in Trinity – though the latter's owner quite reasonably likes his privacy and neither the manor nor the *colombier* is open to public view on a regular basis.

If you leave St Helier by a more northerly route (A7), you pass the architectural jumble of the Hotel de France on the right and Government House on the left and shortly reach a sharp bend at St Saviour's Church. Here in the churchyard we filmed a scene in which a member of the Freemasons was laid to rest. It was an interesting episode, conceived by one of the best writers we have ever had on *Bergerac*, John Fletcher. The central character was a Freemason, played by the admirable Alfred Burke, who was sickened by the infiltration of unscrupulous self-seeking men into the Brotherhood. He decided to punish these transgressors in the name of God by randomly killing them. The story opened with a Masonic initiation ceremony which contains, because of its mediaeval origins, some graphic bloodthirsty language.

We arranged for this initiation ceremony to be shot in an old hall belonging to an educational college quite close to the church. We held rehearsals there, the designers and cameramen went ahead with their preparations, and then like a bolt from the blue permission to film in the hall was withdrawn.

The reason eventually given was that at some time in the past the hall had been used for sacred purposes and some older members of the community might be offended if they saw it being used as a location for a Masonic ceremony played out by actors. This called for some very expensive changes of plan before eventually the scene was shot in a little hall in Ealing. It looked every bit as good as it would have done had it been shot in Jersey; the only difference being that it cost three times as much.

The Masons took a keen interest in that particular episode, inquiring very closely into the nature and content of the piece with the intention, I assumed, of opposing its transmission had it been found to contain anything scandalous or defamatory about their activities. As far as we were concerned it did not do so, beyond suggesting that it was possible for their movement, like many others, to be infiltrated by sinful men keen to use it for their own selfish purposes. At the same time it was salutory to find that surveillance of even a light-hearted cops-and-robbers drama was being carried out not just by Mary Whitehouse but by another, much less visible organisation.

St Saviour's Church, or L'Eglise de St Sauveur de L'Epine (the thorn), may have been built on the site of a much earlier, pre-Christian place of worship. While religious historians justifiably find that a fascinating topic for investigation, the immediate interest of most visitors to the churchyard is captured by a more tangible, and curvaceous, object: the bust which commemorates Jersey's most famous daughter, Emilie Charlotte Le Breton or, as she is better known, Lillie Langtry.

I must confess that I had never understood the claims made for her beauty. Those few photographs I had seen were not impressive, the face seemed ordinary, the figure nondescript. She must have had some remarkable quality to take London society by storm in the 1870s, but I could not then see what it was.

Some years ago, we were shooting some scenes in St Helier in the quaint little area between Pier Road and the Weighbridge. It was a showery day and the delays and

vexations of filming had me looking around for some release from the tedium. I wandered up Pier Road and into the museum of La Société Jersiaise, an excellent and helpful society dedicated to the exploration and celebration of Jersey's past. Inside, I came upon a room to the right of the entrance which is dedicated to the memory of Lillie Langtry and filled with memorabilia of her life and times. There on the south wall hangs a portrait of Lillie by Sir John Millais, and it was a revelation.

Here was the woman who could entrance a whole generation, hold audiences all over the world in the palm of her hand and capture the heart of a prince. It is impossible to describe adequately in words the beauty Millais has captured on canvas: the violet eyes, the astonishing complexion, the determined and coquettishly equivocal gaze. Suffice to say, if you see the painting you may well come to understand how she achieved what she did.

She was born in 1853 into a large family, the only sister to five brothers and later a sixth, in the Old Rectory of St Saviour. Her father was the Dean of Jersey, the Very Revd William Corbet Le Breton. Even as a young girl her beauty was renowned throughout the island and she never lacked for would-be husbands or lovers. But Lillie became enamoured of what she saw as sophisticated society life across the sea in

Another episode by John Fletcher, one of my favourite writers, who is not afraid to confront the big issues. In this case it was freemasonry and I was given the opportunity of working with Alfred Burke, a long-standing hero of mine, whom I remembered and admired from Public Eye, *a very successful series of some years ago.*

Millais's portrait of Lillie Langtry which combines a marvellous sexuality with an intelligence that seems to be overlooked in most other portraits – a potent combination.
BELOW *Edmund Blampied captures the exiled Victor Hugo in typical pose, no doubt gazing across the water from his favourite spot on the St Saviour's waterfront.*

England and, more particularly, London, the great metropolis which at that period of the 19th century had pretensions to being the centre of the universe, let alone the world. That was where she wanted to be.

By marrying a rather pathetic though rich Irish yachtsman, Edward Langtry, she conquered her first great objective. They were married in St Saviour's Church in 1874, and a year later settled in London. There, while her poor husband found society life extraordinarily dull and took himself off on extended fishing expeditions accompanied by a bottle, Lillie was idolised by the smart set. Painters queued up to make portraits of the island beauty, Millais among them. He called his masterpiece *A Jersey Lily* and it is this portrait of her which now hangs in the Pier Road Museum. When it was first shown in the Royal Academy, it had to be cordoned off to save it from being damaged by the hordes who came to admire the painter's art and the lady's beauty.

The radiant Lillie could do no wrong. Her list of close friends included such amazingly disparate stars in the social firmament as Oscar Wilde and William Gladstone, but it was her bizarre liaison with the Prince of Wales, 'Bertie', that most captivated the public.

They had a tempestuous affair, which is probably unsurprising given her great beauty and his notorious libidinous urges. What is remarkable, however, is that their love affair changed over the years into an affectionate life-long friendship. As Edward embarked on other affairs, so Lillie turned to Prince Louis of Battenberg, a handsome naval officer by whom she became pregnant. She returned to Jersey for the birth, and because in those days there was a greater need than now to be seen to preserve high principles of propriety, her daugher, Jeanne Marie, did not learn the identity of her father until she was eighteen.

Lillies's meteoric career in the theatre began as her affair with the Prince of Wales was ending. She was the first society woman to take to the stage and her début, surrounded as it was by the whiff of scandal and more than a touch of the salacious, was hugely successful. She went on to create her own theatrical company, no mean achievement given the temper of the times, and successfully toured both in Britain and the USA. It was while in America that the notorious Judge Roy Bean saw one of her performances. He became so besotted with her that he renamed his town Langtry, which it must be said was a decided improvement on the name it had before, Vinagaroon. Unfortunately Roy Bean died before, in 1904, Lillie came to visit Langtry; unable to meet the extraordinary Judge, she accepted instead the gift of his gold-plated revolver. This piece can now be seen in the Pier Road Museum.

At the age of 46, now divorced from Edward Langtry, Lillie married the 24-year-old Hugo de Bathe. On the death of his father, Hugo became Sir Hugo and Lillie thus ascended to the nobility as Lady de Bathe – the apotheosis of her career in society. This second marriage was also solemnised in St Saviour's Church.

Time eventually took its toll of her beauty and her ambition. After World War I Lillie retired to Monaco. She spent her last years in the principality, and died there in 1929. As Shakespeare wrote of Juliet, 'Beauty too rich for use, for earth too dear.'

Ponterrin Gateway

ST HELIER

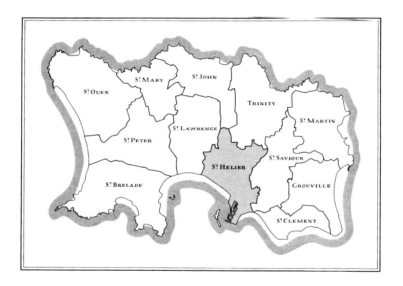

This parish consists largely of the town of St Helier, capital of Jersey, in which about one-third of the island's population live. Surprisingly, perhaps, in view of its proximity to France, it seems a very English town; the reasons for this are not hard to find.

At the end of the Napoleonic Wars Jersey, and St Helier in particular, received a large influx from England of pensioned-off military men and their families. Their arrival and settlement began a process of thoroughgoing anglicisation which had many social consequences. One of the most important was to hasten the death of the Jersey *patois* as the vernacular island tongue. Nowadays the visitor will find only some older people speaking *patois*, and Norman French is reserved for formal occasions, such as before a sitting of the States assembly when prayers are said in French, or when the chamber declares itself 'pour' or 'contre' a motion placed before it.

The houses built for the new arrivals were in the English Regency style, and by the end of the 19th century the English character of St Helier was firmly established. Queen Victoria visited the island in 1846 and a rather unsuccessful statue was erected in 1890 which now stands in the little park on the west side of town near the Grand Hotel. C. E. B. Brett, in his *Buildings in the Town and Parish of St Helier* (1977) wrote that 'she looks like a cross between the Widow Twankey and the White Queen in *Alice in Wonderland*', and it is hard to disagree with this judgment. In general the arrival in force of the English has done little to enhance the beauty of the island's principal town.

Whatever its architectural virtues, or lack of them, St Helier has provided the *Bergerac* team with numerous locations while, in return, our programmes have given the locals plenty of simple amusement. They are particularly pleased when, for example, the magic of film makes it appear that you can enter the tunnel beneath Fort Regent and emerge at the other end into St Brelade, in reality several miles down the road. They love that kind of thing.

Our very own Bureau des Etrangers, before its move to Gorey (see chapter 'St Martin') was located in Royal Square in the States Building which also houses the Royal Court, States Chamber and Library. I cannot remember filming in the chamber more than once, but recommend it as a fine and dignified seat of government. It was built in 1887 in Jacobean style, and from the public gallery visitors can see the beautiful silver mace given by Charles II to Jersey in acknowledgment of the great services rendered to him by the island.

C. E. B. Brett was not so complimentary about the States Building which he saw as being 'uncomfortably like an ancient aircraft

carrier run aground by accident in the Royal Square. Yet it undoubtedly commands the affections of the citizens who like the Royal Square exactly as it is, and no doubt by now it has acquired historical and sentimental associations which are not evident to the outsider.'

In my own view Royal Square is a charming place and holds many pleasant memories. For one of the episodes of *Bergerac* the entire paved area was transformed into an outdoor café with brightly coloured tables and chairs, and a silver band to entertain the multitude. I remember the episode especially well for it featured Greta Scaachi who has since gone on to become a major international star.

One of Jersey's most famous paintings depicts the death in Royal Square of Major Peirson. The original, by John Singleton Copley, hangs in the Tate Gallery, London, and reproductions of it may be seen in many Jersey households; a copy by W. Holyoake is in the Royal Court.

The moment recorded in the painting occurred at the height of the brief but glorious Battle of Jersey in 1781. When the French in 1778 sided with the American revolutionaries against England, Jersey became at war with France. In consequence, French shipping was now fair game for Jersey privateers operating with their *lettres de marque* which authorised them to bring their prizes to the island and were virtually licences to prey on any French ship they found.

The French retaliated by planning an invasion of Jersey. A mercenary adventurer, Baron de Rullecourt, gathered a force of about 1,000 men and prepared to land at La Rocque. This was a highly dangerous assault point, the rocks and reefs forming an almost impenetrable barrier, but de Rullecourt had in his pay a treacherous Jersey pilot, Pierrre Journeaux, who guided the 26 boats of the invasion force through the only navigable channel in the rocks.

The night landing on 5 January was not a complete success. Although the duty militiamen were drunk and not at their posts, de Rullecourt was unable to land men from seven of his boats before the tide turned. This left him with barely 600 men to invade an island guarded by 1,000 regular soldiers and 3,000 militiamen – numbers very much against the odds for an attacking force. For all that, he was a man of resource and advanced on St Helier with 500 of his men. He succeeded in surprising Jersey's Lieutenant-Governor, Major Moyse Corbet, in bed and persuaded him to order his troops to surrender by claiming that his men in St Helier were only part of a massive invading army that was already in virtual control of the island.

Several miles away in the parish of St Peter, Major Francis Peirson was in command of the 95th Foot. On receiving news of the French invasion, he marched his troops to Gallows Hill, now Westmount, and there linked with a mixed force of Highlanders and local militiamen; together they formed a small army about 1,500 strong. Assuming command, Peirson despatched some of his men to Mont de la Ville, where Fort Regent was subsequently built, in order that they could fire down on the enemy in the town.

The main thrust of the counter-attack came along what is now Broad Street and Library Place. Peirson himself led a third detachment up the present King Street precinct and through the Place named after him into the square. The Battle of Jersey lasted all of ten minutes. The French, realising they were hopelessly outnumbered,

Wandering through the streets of Jersey during a break in filming. On my right is Richard Griffiths, a splendidly witty man with whom I had the pleasure of working during my time with the RSC. The observant reader will notice that Richard is wearing a somewhat ornate wig, as this episode was shot shortly after his head had been shaved for his role in the BBC's Cleopatra. *As I remember it was not a very comfortable experience for a large man on a hot day!*

surrendered quickly, though not before both commanders, de Rullecourt and Peirson, were killed. In the parish church a somewhat prosaic monument records that Major Francis Peirson 'died in the flower of youth and in the moment of victory on the sixth day of January 1781 aged 24'.

The harbour at St Helier extends southward from the town in a series of arms, and here we have filmed many times; on one fondly remembered occasion Terence Alexander took an involuntary dip in the marina – an act unfortunately not immortalised on celluloid.

We had been filming an underwater fight sequence at the Minquiers, pronounced locally as the 'Minkies', a group of rocky islets an hour's boat ride from town. Such scenes are always difficult because they involve so many variable factors, among them the position of the boats which is critical for camera angles, the state of the sea surface, visibility below surface, and the obvious problems of communication between director, technicians and actors in a shifting environment.

This particular fight sequence was no exception to the rule and filming dragged on for hours, becoming more and more arduous. We finally finished in the late afternoon and I climbed onto the upper deck of the motor launch to join Terence who had been lounging in the sun all day. He greeted me by saying how pleased he was to have reached that stage of venerable seniority where he did not have to dive into the sea to earn a crust. We arrived back in St Helier as the sun was sinking behind West Hill and Terence, no doubt thinking of a good dinner and a bottle of claret, contrived to miss his footing between the pontoon and the boat and plunged feet first into the unsavoury waters of the marina. He came out dripping to declare, in a not very understated fashion, that he was not best pleased.

As the programme has become more popular over the years, it has grown increasingly difficult to film in St Helier itself. The merest glimpse of a red Triumph Roadster is enough to bring the crowds in their hundreds, blocking the narrow streets,

A bright young WPC (played by Denika Fairman) who taught Bergerac a thing or two during this episode. She seemed to have this clipboard with her in every scene and when we finished filming she presented it to me.

creating even more traffic problems and often preventing the cameraman from getting the shots he wants. From his point of view it is not easy to suggest a quiet urban street when hordes of people are milling about, pressing forward for a better view, taking photographs and making a lot of noise. Nor are these ideal conditions for local people trying to go about their daily business in the town. Nowadays if we must film in St Helier we all – film crew, actors, make-up artists, wardrobe and assorted technicians – sneak furtively into town like so many criminals during the dead hours of Sunday morning when there is never anyone about. Such is the price of success. Before the show was well known we could get away with pretending we were filming a documentary; these apparently interest nobody, and we were left to shoot our scenes in relative peace and quiet.

One day we were at the Grand Hotel for a scene in which Bergerac, dishevelled, unshaven and hungover, had to ask the receptionist what he had been doing the previous evening since he could not remember. 'I was ill last night,' I said by way of explanation.

'And you don't look too well now,' said a real-life lady guest who just happened to have strolled to the desk for her key. 'I'd lie down, love, if I were you,' she added; I felt obscurely flattered that she had not penetrated the pretence for a second.

St Helier is dominated by three edifices. Two were built for warfare and the other, a chimney, was built, I would have thought, to annoy almost anyone who looks at it. The military buildings are Fort Regent, situated on the hill overlooking the town, and Elizabeth Castle which lies offshore near the harbour. The chimney is the flue for La Collette power station: I find it an outstandingly ugly piece of work, made even more so when, unaccountably, it is floodlit at night with green lights.

Fort Regent has recently been converted into a large and impressive sports and leisure complex, though to me it is much more interesting as an outstanding example of defensive military architecture. Although completed too late (1814) to see any action in the Napoleonic Wars, there can be little doubt that had it done so its maze of hugely ingenious interlocking features would have posed enormous problems to an invader.

Town Hill or Mont de Ville had long been recognised as the key to the defence of St Helier. In 1550 the Court of Edward VI issued the following command to the townsfolk: 'Because on occasion of foreign invasion we be informed that you have no place of strength to retire into, we require you to convey your town into the hill above the same, which we be informed may with little charge be made strong and defensible.'

Little or nothing was done at the time, and work on the Fort did not begin until 1806, when the threat of a French invasion spurred the Crown authorities to purchase the land on Mont de Ville from its reluctant owners. In charge of the building operations was Major (later Lieutenant-General) John Hambly Humfrey. The Fort is long and fish-shaped in plan, with the head in the north and the tail in the south. On the long western side Humfrey improved the natural advantage of the steep cliffs by blasting them until they overhung the ground beneath, and built a massive defensive wall. On the eastern side, where the ground slopes more gently, he blasted a deep gorge and built outworks to the north of it which overlooked the entire east-facing side of the Fort. Access to the outworks was by a rolling or retractable bridge and guns mounted there could fire both outwards and, swung sideways, enfilade any closer approaches to the eastern wall. On the south side of the Fort, Humfrey built a formidable glacis, a broad open slope on which the defenders could level a devastating crossfire from the two angled walls facing it. All in all, he assembled a near-impregnable stronghold.

A sample of the entertainment available at Fort Regent.

Fort Regent is fascinating as a military installation and also because it was never tested by an invading enemy. Unlike those heavyweight boxing champions who manage to retire undefeated after several dozen successful defences of their title, Fort Regent held on to its 100 per cent record merely by existing for the better part of two centuries, including World War II when it formed just one link in an all-island chain of defensive positions.

But what if, in the second decade of the 19th century, the French had sailed across the Channel and tried to storm this massive stronghold on the hill above St Helier? Would they have been thrust back into the sea or would they have captured it? The fact that these are unanswerable questions has never deterred zealous military historians from asking them. My own guess, aided by the more precise reasoning of William Davies, architect and military expert, is that the Fort might well have held out for an impressive length of time, very possibly long enough to hope for a relieving action by the Royal Navy.

Let us imagine for a moment that we are 19th-century invaders and have subjugated all of Jersey except for Fort Regent. How would we go about taking this last and most formidable strongpoint?

An attack from the west, perhaps, sweeping up the hill from the harbour? Most unlikely. Beneath the walls of the Fort on that side are steep cliffs, deliberately blasted inwards at the foot, as we have seen, to make a scaling assault still more difficult. An invading force of fully equipped soldiers would have had to climb the cliffs under fire, then mine or overrun the walls on arrival. Meanwhile, they could expect little or no covering fire from their colleagues below. As William Davies has explained, '. . . effective uphill trajectory from cannon was out of the question'. Even if the Fort were bombarded from the far side of the harbour, on the hills above what is now the Inn on

ABOVE *Bergerac at his most athletic and (above right) the moment that they yelled cut and we realised what a compromising position we were all in and wasn't it a rather silly way to earn a living. If you look closely you can see Sean Arnold grinning all over his face, with me in a sandwich between little Brian Capron, pinned to the floor, and the considerably larger Geoffrey Leesley.*

the Park, the western defensive wall is 18 feet thick and would be a stout obstacle to cannon firing from such a distance, in those days close to the limit of their effective range.

From the east an attack would have different, though no less severe, obstacles to overcome. Here Humfrey carried out radical surgery on the gentle natural slope of the hill, blasting the gorge which you can see between Regent Road and the Fort, where the cable cars now run. Add to this the eastern outworks and the cunning disposition of the defensive walls, aligned so that the besieged could fire both outwards and *along* the walls, and you considerably reduce the attackers' chances of success.

Finally, to the south, there is that glacis, Humfrey's solution to an enemy trying to rush the defences from that direction. Although now somewhat obscured by the swimming pool you can still see, stretching down towards South Hill, the long, broad and open space along which the enemy would have had to advance without any form of natural cover, while the defenders pounded him with a terrible concentrated crossfire from the two angled walls at the 'fishtail' or southern extremity of the Fort.

Yes, we can safely say that General Humfrey did his work remarkably well. Should you go there, whether for a swim, a concert or a game of badminton, take time to stroll the ramparts and picture the Fort as it was in its earliest years. The views are great, and, seeing everything at first hand, you can more readily appreciate the fiendish ingenuity of those old-time military engineers.

Fort Regent overlooks, and superseded, the older fortress of Elizabeth Castle which, outmoded though it may be, is a rather splendid prologue to landfall in Jersey. It was built on L'Islet by Paul Ivy, or Ive, in Elizabeth I's reign and was named after

Not just potatoes and Jersey cabbage!

LEFT *In the pleasing St Helier shopping precinct which is usually a little more crowded and (above) holidaymakers who could never get Britain a bad name.*

RIGHT *The gilded statue of George II in Royal Square positioned in 1751, thus making the square 'Royal'. By the 1850s however, it was popularly believed that it was a statue of a Roman Emperor salvaged from a wreck!*
BELOW *Fast food joints and even faster surfers leaving the pounding St Ouen's surf.*

her by Sir Walter Raleigh, then Governor of Jersey, who wrote to her that he wished to call it the 'Castle Fort Isabella Bellissima' (Most Beautiful Elizabeth). The States modified this flowery title to 'le Chasteau Elizabeth' and by 1603 it was generally known by its present name.

A word, by the way, about the parish saint, who first came to public notice on this same islet more than 1,000 years earlier. Helier, also referred to in some places by his Latin name, Helibertus, was a 6th-century religious man said to discipline himself by praying day and night while standing on sharp stones in icy water. When he arrived in Jersey, possibly from Nanteuil in Normandy, he lived in a cave on a rock near L'Islet and became locally famous for his healing powers and for his skill in wrecking pirate ships which threatened the island. He was killed in about 555, either by Saxon pirates or by Vandals from North Africa. In the 12th century an oratory, now called the hermitage, was built on the rock to honour him and on St Helier's Day, or the Sunday closest to 16 July, a pilgrimage is made there and a wreath laid.

The original purpose of Elizabeth Castle was to equip St Helier with a 'modern' strongpoint more capable of withstanding siege by cannon than the medieval Mont Orgeuil Castle at Gorey. Elizabeth Castle was considerably enlarged by Sir Philippe de Carteret between 1626 and 1636, an investment which more than proved its worth in the Civil War. Jersey people tended to support the Parliamentary side, but when the deeply Royalist Sir Philippe took refuge in the Castle he was able to repel the efforts of the local militia while his nephew, Captain George de Carteret, won back the island for the king.

Life in the divided Jersey produced some odd challenges and some equally odd solutions. One of the Royalist commanders of Elizabeth Castle could see his wife, who lived across the water in St Aubin, but could not speak to her without leaving the Castle, which would have been fatal. He therefore devised a code for communicating with her. If she was seen walking along the front, this meant she was in good health and spirits. If she returned to her garden and hung out three sheets on the line, this meant that the news from England was good; if she hung out one, the news was bad; two chemises with a sheet on either side meant there was no news. Unfortunately for the commander the code was discovered before it could be implemented. The name of this ingenious soldier was Porter Hungerford, and I cannot help seeing connections between him and the equally devious Charlie.

Porter Hungerford was a most efficient military man. From Elizabeth Castle he sent marauding parties to capture fishing boats in the bay and attack the town guards in St Helier at night. He fired his guns into the town at all hours and bombarded the Market Square (now Royal Square) on a Saturday afternoon when he knew it would be crowded. Chevalier, a chronicler of the time, described one such attack:

'Bullets fell like thunderbolts all over the market. Some of the terrified people cast themselves on the ground, whilst others in their mad stampede for cover charged and overset every obstacle that came in their way. Stalls were smashed and merchandise scattered in all directions. Money which had been passing from buyer to seller was hurled aside and left where it fell.'

These constant attacks unnerved the people and undermined the Parliamentary opposition to the point that on 21 November 1643 Major Lydcott, the Parliamentary leader, fled and Jersey returned to the Royalist cause with George de Carteret as the new Governor. He held the island for Charles II until 1651 when Parliamentary forces under Admiral Blake landed in St Ouen's Bay and prepared to besiege Elizabeth Castle. This passage from Clarendon's *History of the Rebellion and Civil Wars* describes the scene at the height of the siege:

'When the castle had been besieged three months and the enemy could not approach nearer to plant their ordinance than at least half one English mile, the sea encompassing round more than so far from any land, and it not being possible for any of their ships to come within such a distance, they brought notwithstanding mortar pieces of such incredible greatness as has never been seen in this part of the world, that from the highest point of the hill, they shot granadoes of a vast bigness into the castle and beat down many houses; and at last blowed up a great magazine where most of the provisions of victuals lay and killed many men. Upon which Sir George Carteret sent an express to give the King an account of the condition he was in and to desire a supply of men and provisions, which it being impossible for his majesty to procure he sent him orders to make the best conditions he could.'

A rare picture of Charlie Hungerford doing his own shopping.

The end was not long in coming. With the abbey church blown up, and most of the gunpowder and provisions destroyed, de Carteret was having to urge his reluctant garrison to their posts at sword point. Seeing that further resistance was futile, he surrendered and Jersey returned to Parliamentary control until the Restoration.

The various layers of fortification added over the centuries to Elizabeth Castle have provided the BBC with a wonderful location, and some of our most successful episodes have been filmed there. The latest was the 1987 Christmas Special with Peter Jeffrey and Liza Goddard. On screen, the film works remarkably well as a light-hearted comedy; the making of it, however, was far from funny, particularly on one memorable day's shooting.

Our plan for the day was to film the *dénouement* of the plot when the ex-policeman (Peter Jeffrey) reveals himself as a villain, shoots Philippa Vale (Liza Goddard), has a fight with Bergerac and then flees towards the oratory only to fall over the cliff and do himself mortal damage. Pretty straightforward stuff, we confidently assumed, but the day started badly.

Charlie Hungerford in full flight along the causeway with Elizabeth Castle in the background.

First of all Goddard's dog, a talented actor in its own right which had appeared with some distinction on the stage, made the mistake of eating some food thrown out by the caterers. The poor dog was very sick indeed, but it was not so much that she was sick as where she was sick that boded ill. The director, a very senior and august person, affected a Roman stoicism as he cleaned Gert's regurgitations from a new pair of shoes acquired only that morning, but no-one seriously doubted that the prospects for a happy day's work had been compromised.

The dog was wrapped in a blanket from the wardrobe department and her mistress went out into a bitter March morning to film the part of the final scene in which she

The harbour at St Helier provides a typical Bergerac setting.

had to run like a bat from the underworld along the breakwater to the south of the Castle. The first time she attempted to run, she was so far from being warmed up that she pulled a muscle in each leg. When I arrived, later, having gone to the wrong embarkation point, I found the lady and her dog both huddled round the one-bar electric fire in wardrobe, the dog waiting for Nature's cure and her owner munching painkillers. These seemed to have the required effect because an hour or so later she and Peter Jeffrey were out on the breakwater filming the middle bit of the scene where he shoots her and takes the diamonds, then looks up and sees Bergerac approaching, fights with him and then legs it towards the oratory.

In the course of this piece of action Peter managed to drop the bag of diamonds on Liza's face, then followed this by accidentally allowing his heavy service revolver to fall on the same target. Liza walked off, accompanied by wardrobe ladies, angels and ministers, sat on a small collapsible chair and probably thought how much better off she would be with Lionel Blair in the warmth and blessed safety of a television studio.

By and large things were not going well. Liza's part of the scene was postponed on humanitarian grounds and Bergerac and Peter got down to the nitty-gritty of the fight. Peter, who is normally the kindest and gentlest of men, continued his pattern of inflicting superfluous pain on his fellow actors. Halfway through our contest he thumped me full on the nose. If he had thumped me anywhere else it might have been bearable, but now the sight of tears running down the hero's cheeks caused the already strained director to shout 'Cut' in a tone of exquisite contempt. The scene was set up again. The weather meanwhile had definitely got colder. The cameraman, Kevin, or

Ripples as he is known thanks to his extraordinarily muscular physique, heaved the camera onto his shoulders and was about to shoot when it became clear that something was unfeignedly wrong with the sound recordist. He was stretched full-length along a low wall and holding his head. Later, after he had been carried away in the direction of the one-bar electric fire, we learned that he was suffering from food poisoning.

We managed to complete the day with no further mishaps but it was a much chastened group of people who thankfully drove back along the causeway to the pubs, wine bars and restaurants of St Helier and beyond. It was little comfort at the time to reflect that Elizabeth Castle and its surrounds have never been noted as a comfortable place of work, whether for soldiers, pirates, hermits or actors.

Old Pier Head

ST LAWRENCE

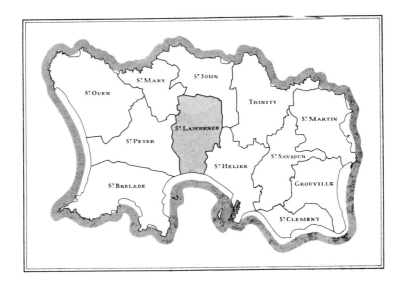

During the Occupation by the Germans Jersey became a huge fortress. Even today the gaunt reminders of those terrible five years are clearly visible, the great grey sea walls, built to stop tanks moving up from the beach, the bunkers and observation posts.

Nowhere was safe from the schemes of the invader. Bastions from a previous era, the Castles of Mont Orgueil and Elizabeth, were both strengthened and refortified. The islanders suffered severe privations through shortage of food and medical supplies, particularly during the last seven months of the war in Europe when, ironically, Jersey was besieged by the British fleet, whose object was to starve the Channel Island garrisons into surrender.

The islanders' situation would have been even more grim had not Lord Portsea, formerly Sir Bertram Falle, a true Jerseyman, managed to impress on the British Government the absolute need to send a relief ship to Jersey. So it was that on 30 December 1944 the good ship *Vega* arrived with 750 tons of food. Joy was unbounded. A fitting memorial to this event may be seen in the Royal Square in St Helier. It was put there by a stonemason, Le Guyader, who was given the task of relaying the flagstones in part of the square. By changing the pattern of the stones, he managed first to form the letter V for victory, and then the entire name Vega without the Germans noticing; the memorial survives today.

The resilient spirit of the islanders manifested itself in many odd ways during this dark period, for example in the design of the new Occupation postage stamps. Major N. V. C. Rybot was ordered to design a stamp which would replace the old British one. In each of the four corners of the new penny stamp he put a very small letter A, and on the halfpenny issue the letters AABB. The meaning of the letters remained a mystery to many until after the war when the Major revealed that the four As on the penny issue stood for Ad Avernum Adolf Atrox, which roughly translated means 'Go to hell, atrocious Adolf.'

The two Bs on the halfpenny stamp stood for Bloody Benito, whose quick passage to the nether regions was also imperatively required.

In the parish of St Lawrence is one of the more terrible memorials to Nazism, the Underground Hospital. Originally intended to provide a barracks and workshops, it was redesigned as a hospital after the Allied invasion of Normandy in 1944. In its melancholy way it is an impressive structure. Some 14,000 tons of rock were quarried to make its long tunnels and 4,000 tons of concrete were used to line their walls. To build it was the task of the Organisation Todt, and slave labour was shipped to the island from all over Europe, mainly from Russia, whence the poor wretches came crammed in unheated, dark and noisome trucks, some to die and others to suffer unspeakable horrors creating this monstrous and strange underground cave, which was still uncompleted at the Liberation. If you are not feeling depressed when you enter this ungodly place, it is a certainty that you will be by the time you leave. Everything in it bespeaks a debased and corrupting view of humanity that freezes the spirit as it offends the mind.

There are many books on that period which lay out a picture of the times in graphic detail, but for me one of the most moving records is the collection of etchings and sketches of the Todt workers by the famous Jersey artist and master craftsman Edmund Blampied. Most of his sketches and paintings are glorious celebrations of humanity, its humour, its love, its joy, and he expresses these qualities best in his many portrayals of the human face, but in these works one scarcely sees the faces at all, they are hidden, closed or covered as if all identity, hope of life and a future had been taken from them.

This is not the place for a detailed account of those years of Occupation. I rather think that only someone who was actually in Jersey and lived through the horror and dreadful events of that time can speak of them with any authority. We who have not

Two wartime designs by Edmund Blampied.
TOP *Jean le Bean, the archetypal Jerseyman, and an old Jersey lady deep in conversation, probably in patois – this was used on the 1/- note during the Occupation.*
ABOVE *The 3d stamp: the elaborate base included a V for victory and the cipher G R as a gesture of defiance.*
RIGHT *Blampied's moving portrayal of the pitifully starved and ragged Todt workers.*

known at first hand the gross nature of military occupation may only guess at the indignity and humiliation, the fury and the pain, the pity and the waste endured by those who did.

Some light in the encircling gloom emerges from John Lewis's marvellous book, *A Doctor's Occupation*, an account of his experiences as a doctor in the island during the Occupation. With food at a premium every new litter of piglets had to be registered with a German official and a strict watch was kept on the numbers of animals up to the time they were slaughtered. If a piglet died, this was recorded by the authorities and, came the next slaughtering day, one less pig would be expected. The Jersey farmer, though, was as guileful then as he is now and for a time the death of one of the litter became a very profitable event. On the demise of a pig, a certificate was obtained from the appropriate German officer. The dead pig was then whisked away surreptitiously to another farmer who in turn reported that one of his pigs had died; a second certificate was issued. This operation was repeated up to four or five times, the same number of certificates being issued to different farmers for just one dead pig. Each farmer in possession of a certificate could thus keep one pig from his litter for his own consumption. As a piece of communal self-help, it takes some beating.

There were even more lugubrious happenings. John Lewis recounts the story of the French whores who were shipped in by the German High Command in the autumn of 1941 to minister to the sexual needs of the troops. The brothel was established at the Hotel Victor Hugo and the rather unsavoury and unattractive women, most of whom were over fifty, settled in, for the duration it was thought. However, the libidinous urges of the conquering Germans seem to have been over-estimated and the turnover of clients never came up to expectations. After a year, the decision was taken to return the 'girls' to France, and to that end they were taken aboard a coaster under a Dutch captain. Outward bound, just off Corbière, the ship struck a rock and foundered.

ABOVE RIGHT *Millbrook House,*
an attractive setting for Bergerac
on several occasions.
ABOVE *A Jersey stone cottage.*
These houses built in the
vernacular style and situated
in a quiet part of the island
like St Lawrence are now
at a premium.

Within minutes she was lost to view. For some little time the women's bodies, their peroxide hair streaming out behind them, could be seen floating in the sea. As Lewis remarks, the sight was infinitely pathetic and saddening.

Hard though those times were the fate of this pretty little island might easily have been worse than it was. In the aftermath of Von Stauffenberg's failed bomb attempt on Hitler's life, many officers who belonged to the old Junker class were replaced by thorough-going Nazis, whose loyalty to Hitler was unquestioned. So it was in Jersey. The German commander in the island, Oberst Graf Rudolf Von Schmettow, was removed from office and replaced by Vice-Admiral Huffmeier, who was determined to carry on the war from Jersey against increasingly impossible odds. Addressing his troops in the now demolished Forum Cinema in Grenville Street, he declared, 'The first duty of the fortress is not to be captured by the enemy. I mean to hold out here with you, till the victory is won.'

His defiance went further than mere words for he launched a very successful assault on Granville, on the Normandy Coast, then held by the Americans. The US forces were quite unprepared for an attack from this quarter and suffered considerable losses. Even after Hitler's suicide in the Berlin bunker, when his successor Admiral Dönitz ordered all German forces to surrender, Huffmeier wanted to continue the war, thereby exposing his troops and, more importantly, the islanders to continued deprivation and mortal danger. His officers, however, opposed his belligerent lunacy and forcefully persuaded him to order a complete and absolute surrender of the island fortress to Brigadier Snow aboard HMS *Beagle*. The date, 9 May 1945, is remembered to this day with great joy by all Jerseymen.

The Jerseyman's attitude now towards the war years is a potent mixture of revulsion and fascination. At the base of the cliffs at Les Landes, to the south of the huge observation tower, lie many guns visible at low water, thrown there by German POWs watched over by British Tommies. They are huge pieces, and on close inspection they appear to be intact. An effort was made recently to lift these monster relics by helicopter to the clifftop. I went to see the results of the operation. It had not been a success: a few small bits and pieces, scarcely recognizable as being parts of a gun, had been deposited in a heap on the clifftop. The huge intact guns had proved too heavy to lift and remained where they had lain for 43 years. I met some old Jersey folk up there who had lived through the Occupation and we talked about it. They all thought that it would be best if the guns were left to lie where they had been flung in what seemed to them a great symbolic gesture, and not dragged back up to help turn Les Landes into a World War II Theme Park! This, they felt, would only cheapen their memories. I am a foreigner here but I see their point . . .

St Lawrence today is a quiet, uncommercialised parish in which it is extremely pleasant to ride out, as the locals say, or bike out as I do, or simply walk which is perhaps best of all. The prettiest place to do any of these things is Waterworks Valley, which is as beautiful an area as any in the island. As the name implies, the Jersey New Waterworks Company have been at work and the three reservoirs, Millbrook, Dannemarche and Handois, are the fruits of their endeavours. The waterworks buildings, the pump houses and so forth, are in a style best thought of as Victorian Industrial and have absolutely nothing to recommend them from an aesthetic point of view, but beyond these and in the north of the valley, it is beautifully quiet and peaceful (except of course when the BBC film car chases along the roads, though this happens but seldom).

Near the top of the valley is Hamptonne Manor, a somewhat subdued example of the vernacular style but boasting a rather splendid and unusual square *colombier*, rebuilt in 1674. My good friend and fictional boss, Sean Arnold, alias Inspector Crozier, lives close to this valley, and so it is that I have had occasion to wander about St Lawrence, savouring its many delights and usually ending up with a pint of the best at the village pub in Carrefour Selous. There the food, at the time of writing, is lusty, the atmosphere smoky and jovial (at least in the public bar) and the talk mostly in genuine Jersey accents!

Morel Farm.

ME AND THE POLICE

During the course of my seven years in Jersey I have come into memorable contact with Jersey's 'real' police force on three occasions. Two of these encounters reflected little glory on me, and the other incident had a tragic outcome.

When I lived at 'Gorseland', in the parish of St Brelade, I used to bathe at Beau Port in the early morning before going to work. One fine summer's day, about 7.30 am, I arrived on the beach. There was not a soul to be seen, but what I did see was a line of footprints leading to a neatly folded pile of male clothing and thence to the water's edge. This intrigued me because in all the years I had lived nearby, I had never known anyone else take a swim at that hour. I looked out to sea for a sight of the swimmer. No-one. I walked to the opposite end of the beach to look round the corner of the bay in both directions but there was still no sign of anyone. Thoughts of Stonehouse, an accident, a suicide filled my head. I tried to dismiss them as fanciful, but time was slipping by.

I had been on the beach for about half an hour and no swimmer had returned. Although it was summer the water was still quite chilly, and half an hour was a long time for someone to stay out there. I decided to raise the alarm. It took a quarter of an hour to get up the cliff path and reach a telephone to dial 999. After listening patiently to my somewhat breathless account of events, the sergeant made the expected inquiry – was I perhaps confusing reality with a *Bergerac* script? Nevertheless he promised to send an officer out to Beau Port. It was nearly nine o'clock when he arrived and the

BELOW *Looking out across Beau Port towards St Brelade's Bay.*
BELOW RIGHT *The two gentlemen assisting Geoffrey Leesley are from the local force. In nearly all cases we use real policemen as extras. You can always recognise them because they are better dressed than we are and act more realistically.*

sun was by now very hot indeed. The policeman was wearing regulation heavy motor-cycle clothing and I suspect he was not best pleased to have to scramble down the cliff path to the beach to check my story. The clothes were still there, as were the foot-prints, but still no bather. We scrambled over the rocks at the edge of the bay but discovered nothing and nobody.

The alarm was then well and truly raised. An ambulance and patrol cars were summoned to the scene and the inshore lifeboat was scrambled. I drove off to work and left them to it. Towards lunchtime I returned to the car park overlooking the bay to find it thronged with vehicles and rescue personnel. They had found no-one, but now were assuming that something untoward must have taken place.

Two days later, having heard nothing in the interim, I happened to meet the patrolman who had first come out to Beau Port when he arrived on the *Bergerac* set as an extra. I asked him if they had found the swimmer. 'Oh yes,' he replied, 'he turned up.' Apparently he had gone off from the beach, swum around the headland to the south-west, sunbathed for a few hours in one of the secluded little coves and then returned. Understandably perhaps, he was not exactly overjoyed to find a uniformed reception committee awaiting him. He was even less overjoyed because it was the second time that month it had happened to him. If by some chance he reads this I offer him my sincere apologies.

My second police clash happened this way. Super-sleuth Bergerac is abed, sleeping soundly. Directly beneath his open bedroom window, all of ten feet away, two bicycles – one his, the other his daughter's – are leaning against the wall. Two young villains making their escape after a particularly nasty attack on a householder at Red Houses, St Brelade, nick the bikes and pedal off. Does wonder-cop, using his legendary talents and highly developed senses, hear anything or notice anything amiss? Not a bit of it. He sleeps through the whole incident and, moreover, takes two days to notice that the bicycles are missing. Some detective, as was made clear to me when I went to the police station to claim the recovered bikes.

The last instance occurred one night some years ago, but I remember what happened so clearly it might have been yesterday.

It was midnight and I was about to go to bed when a ring sounded at the door. I assumed it would be some jolly actors or a couple of locals dropping in for a drink, but there at the door were two teenagers imploring me to get help because someone had fallen off the cliff. I quickly phoned the police and then drove my car along the rough track to the clifftop. I rushed down the cliff path towards the rocks at the bottom and immediately it was clear what had happened.

I found a man, stripped to the waist, staring out to sea and sobbing, and every so often shouting out his friend's name. This friend had been fishing from a little place nearby and for some reason had slipped and plunged 25 feet into the sea and disappeared. He just had time to explain this before the police and rescue service arrived in force with cars, firetenders and ambulances. In an amazingly short space of time they had rows of powerful lamps shining from the clifftop out over the sea where the unfortunate man had disappeared, and at the foot of the cliffs thirty or forty men formed a great horseshoe shape around the cove and shone their torches over the inshore waters. Apart from the waves washing against the dark rocks and the distant throb of diesel engines out to sea, there was no noise, everyone was very quiet, watching, straining to see, hoping for the smallest sign of life. It never came. The man's body was later found a hundred yards out to sea by one of the search vessels. He had hit his head in the fall down the rocks and was dead when he hit the water.

We left the cliff-face in the early hours of the morning. It had been a miserable experience: each one of us present, by witnessing one man's mortality, had been made uncomfortably aware of his own.

Etchings by **MICHAEL RICHECOEUR**

These etchings appear on the opening pages of each parish

St Brelade: **LA COTTE**

A view across St Brelade's Bay looking out towards La Cotte, the scene of several excavations which have yielded extraordinary results in terms of mammoth and also human remains. There was obviously a remarkably developed and sophisiticated settlement there for many years. It is probably the richest excavation site in Jersey but is totally inaccessible to the public.

St Peter: **LA ROCCO**

It was originally planned that La Rocco Tower be built entirely by local labour and every mason in the country was asked to give so much work per week. This was not so bad if you lived in St Ouen, but if you came from the other side of the island, from St Martin or Grouville, the idea did not greatly appeal, and so it took an unconscionable length of time to build. This was also one of the four proposed sites for a deep-water harbour but the rocky nature of this part of the coast and the strength of the tides ruled it out and St Catherine's was eventually chosen.

St Ouen: **ST OUEN'S MANOR**

St Mary: **BOULES AU MOULIN**

Jersey as Michael Richecoeur would like it to be. All Jersey folk and no cars. Cars never feature in Michael's work nor do undressed figures. His characters are always well clothed as most Jersey people are. Like so many other islanders they take little interest in swimming and watersports.

St John: **COTIL**

The Jersey farmers have a most sensible way of ploughing these fields. They anchor a tractor at the top of the slope and run the plough up and down on a system of wires and pulleys. This picture is set above Bonne Nuit Bay.

Trinity: **BOULEY BAY**

St Martin: **ANCHORAGE**

If you go out to the Ecrehous on a Sunday you will find them covered with Jersey people drinking copious amounts of wine and eating the delicious lobsters. You will also find the Union Jack flying, to remind the neighbouring French of the ownership of the islands. The birds nest right under your feet so you have to be very careful where you walk and the narrow passage of water in the foreground of Michael Richecoeur's etching is alive with fish and other sea-life. The houses on the Ecrehous are privately owned by Jersey families and there are no facilities for other visitors.

Grouville: **QUEEN'S FARM**

St Clement: **ORMERING**
I have only ever tasted ormers once. They are small shellfish which became extremely rare. They are now being reintroduced into Jersey waters in marketable quantities and are a great delicacy, or are regarded as such by the islanders although, personally, I am in no hurry to try them again. It would seem scarcity adds flavour to the feast.

St Saviour: **LE DICQ**
St Saviour's pathway to the sea. Every parish must have access to the sea but St Saviour's ration of coastline is limited to just 10 yards, and here it was that Victor Hugo is supposed to have sat and gazed across at France during his stay on the island.

St Helier: **ST HELIER**
The tower of La Collette power station and Fort Regent, neither of which are greatly admired by Michael Richecoeur, are perhaps deliberately reduced to secondary roles in the background of this picture. The foreground is understandably given to two more favoured landmarks – the Oratory chapel, on the right, and, at the other end of the causeway, Elizabeth Castle.

St Lawrence: **SERIOUS CRIB**
Another picture of Jersey life as it should be, with a certain amount of artistic licence. Carrefour Selous is one of the principal inland crossroads but Michael sees it as it was and as he would like it to be – hardly a roadway in sight and certainly no transport.

EDMUND BLAMPIED
1886–1966

Edmund Blampied was a very prolific painter and, very much like Michael Richecoeur, he turned his back on almost certain international success in his own lifetime and returned to Jersey because, I believe, he felt that being away from the island divorced him from the source of his inspiration – the place that he knew, understood and could portray artistically. He was a charming, shy and, on occasions, somewhat mischievous man with a lovely sense of humour and a detestation of modern abstract art. His portrayal of Jersey life owes at least as much to his love of the place as to his considerable technical ability. So prolific was he that his work is still found all over the island. I once went to see my landlady who said she thought she had a Blampied; she wasn't sure whether she had or not but went into her lavatory and took this rather mildewed picture off the wall. It was indeed a Blampied. She was totally unaware of the value of the painting, to her it was just a pretty picture of Jersey.

I am extremely grateful to the Société Jersiaise and the Jersey Museums Service for their permission to reproduce the following illustrations from their collection:–

BIBLIOGRAPHY

Ahier, P. *Jersey Sea Stories* (Advertiser Press, Huddersfield, 1957)

Balleine, G.R. *The Tragedy of Philippe d'Auvergne* (Phillimore, 1973)

Balleine, G.R. *All For The King* (Société Jersiaise, 1976)

Birkitt & Richardson, *Lillie Langtry* (John Richardson, 1985)

Brett, C.E.B. *Buildings in the Town and Parish of St Helier* (Ulster Architectural Heritage Society, 1977)

Davies, W. *Fort Regent, A History* (St Helier, Jersey)

Davies, W. *The Harbour That Failed* (printed privately)

Eagleston, A.J. *The Channel Islands Under Tudor Government* (Cambridge, 1949)

Layzell, A. *Announcing the Arrival* (Channel Television, 1987)

Lemprière, R. *Customs, Ceremonies & Traditions of the Channel Islands* (Robert Hale, 1976)

Lewis, J. *A Doctor's Occupation* (New English Library, 1985)

McCormack, J. *Channel Island Churches* (Phillimore, 1986)

Ramsey, W.G. *The War in the Channel Islands*

Rybot, N.V.L. *Elizabeth Castle* (Société Jersiaise, 1986)

Stevens, J. *Old Jersey Houses* Vols I and II (Société Jersiaise, 1972)

Stevens, J. *Victorian Voices* (Société Jersiaise, 1969)

Syvret, M. *Edmund Blampied* (Robin Garton Ltd, 1986)

Syvret, M. & Stevens, J. *Balleine's History of Jersey* (Phillimore, 1981)

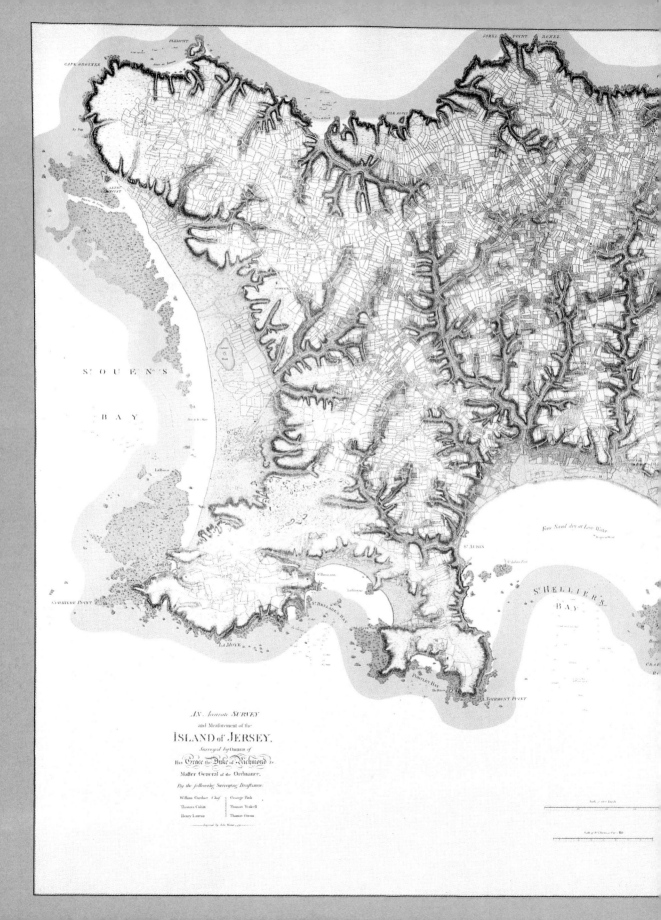

AN Accurate SURVEY
and Measurement of the
ISLAND of JERSEY,
Surveyed by ORDER of
His Grace the Duke of Richmond &c.
Master General of the Ordnance,
By the following Surveying Draftsmen.

William Gardner Chief	George Bink
Thomas Gilbert	Thomas Yeakell
Henry Lauran	Thomas Owens